Making

BIG
Money
in
Small
Stocks

**Beat the Street
with Stocks under $5**

by
Bill Mathews

William —

Have fun, make money and enjoy my book

Bill Mathews

Library of Congress Cataloging
Making Big Money in Small Stocks / Bill Mathews
ISBN 0-9745875-0-8

This book is designed to provide information on investment strategies. It is sold with the understanding that the publisher and author are not engaged in rendering legal, accounting or other professional services. If legal or other expert assistance is required, the services of a competent professional should be sought.

Every effort has been made to make this book as complete and as accurate as possible. However, there may be mistakes, both typographical and in content. Therefore, this text should be used only as a general guide and not as the ultimate source of investing information.

The purpose of this book is to educate and entertain. The author and Mathews & Associates shall have neither liability nor responsibility to any person or entity with respect to any loss or damage caused, or alleged to have been caused, directly or indirectly, by the information contained in this book.

Preface

My primary reason for writing *Making BIG Money in Small Stocks* is to help you become the best investor you can be. Statistics indicate that 70 percent of all investors lose money in the stock market. Why? Most investors buy poor quality stocks at too high a price. They either get greedy and don't take their profit, or ignore signals that indicate the price may go down. Then they end up selling their stocks for a loss. This book will give you a better understanding of the stock market in general, and how to pick quality stocks, buy them at a good low price and sell for a tidy profit.

My investing philosophy has worked both in good markets and bad. Basically, I look for a company that's fundamentally solid, with increasing sales and earnings that is selling near its 52-week low price. In its simplest form, it's finding the bargain. I've used that philosophy successfully for over 25 years, and call it the "CHEAP" philosophy.

Almost everyone has heard the old adage, "Buy low and sell high". Logically, that is the only way an investor will make money. The problem most investors have is they don't think for themselves. Instead, they follow the herd. They get caught up in momentum buying, where they buy a stock that has hit new highs on the assumption that it will keep going higher. While momentum buying works well during bull markets, investors who followed that strategy after March 2000 through 2002, lost gigantic sums of money.

Investors now realize that investment strategies, like momentum investment, which worked in the bull market of the 90s, may not make the grade in today's more uncertain market. Political upheaval, terrorism, and accounting irregularities in the billions of dollars have caused an edgy market to become ever more volatile. Where should the investor turn? Back to the basics.

Looking back over 25 years of various investment strategies touted by different experts, the one strategy that I've seen work in both good markets and bad is buying low and selling high. J. Paul Getty stated it best in his well-known book, *How to be Rich*. He wrote that an investor should "Buy when everyone else is selling and sell when everyone is buying. This is more than a catchy slogan. It is the very essence of successful investing and accumulating wealth."

Quality, low priced stocks are very attractive to the small investor because they have the potential for huge profits. However, it is vital that you invest in a company that has solid fundamentals AND purchase the stock at the right price. Would you purchase an automobile for $45,000 that was selling for $30,000 just last week? No, you wouldn't because it's too expensive! It's common sense, but too many investors get caught up in the excitement of investing and jump on the bandwagon to purchase a great little stock, which just doubled in price. Sound familiar? We hear it all the time. Doesn't it make more sense to get into that stock before it skyrockets? That's what you'll learn to do if you follow the techniques in the book.

Recently I watched some experts on CNBC issue buy recommendations on stocks they believed were good investments. One expert liked CarMax at $39. CarMax (KMX) is a great stock, but I liked it a lot better when I recommended it in my newsletter at $1.56. As usual, Wall Street finally discovered a stock after my subscribers had already made a 2,400 percent profit! Another expert liked Bradley Pharmaceuticals (BDY) at $31.50. I recommended that one at $1.03. My subscribers had almost a 3,000 percent profit by the time Wall Street liked the stock. Not only buying a quality stock, but also waiting for that stock price to drop to an attractive level is what makes my investment strategy so successful. You have to be in the right stock AT THE RIGHT PRICE to routinely make good profits on your investments.

Of course it's important to analyze the company before buying its stock. It used to be a time-consuming, tedious job to write or call a company for information to help you determine if the stock had investment potential. That changed with the advent of the Internet. With the click of a button, the Internet allows investors access to the current price and background information on almost any company. Where previously, analysts were the only ones who had such data at their fingertips, the Internet has become the great equalizer. The sudden availability of huge amounts of information has given everyone the chance to be a stock guru.

However, the Internet is a two-edged sword. While it is easier than ever before to learn about a potential investment, it has also caused information overload. Add chat lines, 24-hour financial networks, financial magazines, and newspapers to the mix, and it's no wonder that investors are feeling overloaded and confused. We've gone from a dearth of information to the extreme of too much information to decipher. Our task has become one of picking through a haystack of data to find (and recognize) the important needles of information. In many cases, we just get overwhelmed and end up doing nothing, because we don't know how to proceed.

If you have this problem, this book is for you! It will detail how to research, sort through the data and analyze it, to find those investment candidates with good profit potential. Over the years, I've learned that I can't know everything. If I try to analyze every stock, I'll just end up frustrated, knowing a little about a lot. Instead, I specialize in one area, stocks under $5. Doing so eliminates the vast majority of information clutter. That frees me to concentrate on one important goal - finding a bargain.

I believe that knowledge is power. This book will give you the tools to make your own educated decision on whether or not to purchase a stock. You won't have to rely on someone else, who may be more interested in a commission than in the quality of the investment. *Making BIG Money in Small Stocks* will teach you to analyze a stock on your own, determine a good price for stock purchase, and how to recognize and protect your profit.

By purchasing this book you've taken the first step. Now make sure that you invest the time and effort to accomplish your goals. After reading this book, you will have a better understanding of the stock market, the economy and the investment process. You'll have the knowledge to buy quality, low-priced stocks. This is the best investment strategy to fulfill your financial dreams!

I welcome your comments on the book and hope you find *Making BIG Money in Small Stocks* interesting, educational and profitable!

Bill Mathews, Editor
The CHEAP Investor
Mathews and Associates, Inc.
2549 West Golf Road, Suite 350
Hoffman Estates, IL 60194
(847) 697-5666
(847) 697-5699 - fax
Website: www.bigmoneysmallstocks.com

Dedications

To Karen, my wife, partner and best friend. This book is a reality because of your hard work and determination. Thank you.

To Allison, Alexander, Jennifer, Kaitlyn, Mallory, Meghan, Olivia and Stephanie. I hope that *Making BIG Money in Small Stocks* is an inspiration to show that with a goal, hard work and perseverance your dreams can come true.

Thank you to Adrienne for proofing, Kat for editing and introducing me to style sheets, and a special thanks to Garrett who created an outstanding book cover.

Table of Contents

Chapter

1

Investing – The National Pastime

Congratulations! You have already joined the ranks of smart investors by purchasing this book to learn how to invest before you actually purchase stock. Taking the time to learn the basics greatly increases your chances of success because, surprisingly, most investors jump headlong into the market without first learning how to play the game.

The United States is unique in that an amazingly large amount of wealth has been accumulated in a relatively short period of time. Our free enterprise system allows clever, industrious individuals to make a fortune. The basic freedoms and opportunities that many Americans take for granted are the enticement for most immigrants to leave everything they know to come to a new country.

Anyone can participate in our free enterprise system by starting a company and becoming a direct owner. However, because most people don't have the necessary capital or entrepreneurial skills, they can indirectly share in the growth and prosperity of a company by investing in its common stock. An investor with a small amount of money can become a partial owner of a growing corporation and enjoy some of the same benefits as the entrepreneur.

While the Japanese hold the record for being compulsive savers, the U.S isn't even in the top 20 nations for savings. However, Americans have a passion for investing, as over 50 percent of U.S. households own stocks. This certainly qualifies investing as a national pastime.

BEFORE YOU INVEST

With your first stock purchase, you will join more than 80 million other Americans, from all walks of life, who own stock in U.S. businesses. Making money from buying and selling stocks is an exciting proposition. Before you begin, however, you must ask yourself if you are ready to invest. You should take a hard look at your financial situation, and any investments you already own, to determine the amount of capital you can afford to invest. Remember - any investment involves some degree of risk, so the funds you have earmarked should be money that you can afford to lose.

When I devised the CHEAP investment philosophy I originally targeted small investors who only had a few thousand dollars. Over the years, I've spoken to many investors who shared their success stories. Several revealed that they used the CHEAP strategy for large purchases and it worked well. I've even had a few callers who bought shares in each stock that I recommended in my newsletter. While it takes a large amount of capital to invest in 3 or 4 stocks each month, they reported that it proved very profitable.

There are many ways to invest. Some like to purchase stock each month. Others only buy one stock each year. Many investors buy low-priced stocks almost exclusively. Others only invest a small portion of their portfolio in low-priced stocks. Most small investors fall someplace between those extremes. The learning point is to realize that you can adapt the CHEAP philosophy to your own situation and desires.

THE BIRTH OF THE CHEAP PHILOSOPHY

I grew up in a large family, and learned at a very early age, that if I wanted something, I had to figure out a way to earn the money to buy it. I got my first paper route at age 10. While most of the money went to my family, each week I would save some in a jar. I was fascinated to watch that money grow week by week.

My foster father, who worked at AT&T, came home one day with an option to buy a few shares of company stock. With such a large family, he wasn't interested in the option, but I was. I asked him to invest my money in the stock. I poured over each AT&T statement, and was thrilled to see my investment grow as the stock price moved upward.

A few years later, I saved enough money to invest in another stock. I found a broker, and he was impressed that I already owned AT&T shares. At that time, AT&T was selling at $63 per share. It was the most profitable company in the country.

As an avid admirer of the automobile industry, I was interested in American Motors, which produced several very innovative and exciting cars. (Chrysler bought American Motors many years ago.) When I called my broker to buy some American Motors stock, he tried to persuade me to give up what he considered as a foolish notion. He had a hard time understanding why I wanted to diversify. He strongly suggested that I put the rest of my money in AT&T, because he thought it was the highest-quality blue chip stock available, and would therefore be my best investment. He assumed that American Motors was on the verge of bankruptcy as it had just set a new record for the largest loss suffered by any company.

When he realized that he couldn't talk me out of my "crazy idea", he asked me to sign a statement indicating that he had not recommended buying American Motors. I signed the statement, and he bought the stock. Even though I invested the same amount of money in American Motors that I did in AT&T, because it was only $3 compared to $63, I was able to buy 21 times as many shares.

Six months later AT&T dropped from $63 to $48 (-24 percent), but American Motors rose from $3 to $13 (+333 percent)! It didn't matter that AT&T was a profitable and highly respected blue chip, and that American Motors had recorded the largest loss in its history. The relative profit and loss percentage was all that mattered. I learned a valuable lesson, one that changed my life forever. From that point on, I always questioned investing in a company just because it was a blue chip. Although I didn't know what a turnaround stock was, when I invested in American Motors, I soon learned.

As I continued to develop my investment philosophy, I realized that I achieved much of my success by acting contrary to the recommendations of Wall Street and the media. In essence, I became a successful investor, not by following the crowd, but by challenging it. These experiences, along with my teaching and research, formed the foundation of the CHEAP philosophy.

CORNERSTONES OF THE CHEAP PHILOSOPHY

I originally developed the CHEAP philosophy in response to my personal investment experiences. With 15 years of teaching college level investment courses, I tested, modified and refined this philosophy. The philosophy has become the cornerstone of my newsletter, *The CHEAP Investor,* which tens of thousands of investors across the country have successfully used since 1981. Over the years I outlined these 13 rules to successful investing.

1. *An educated investor is a successful investor.* Let's face it, no one has as much interest as you do in seeing your money grow. Your best strategy is to educate yourself about the investing process, so you can make intelligent decisions. You don't buy a house without checking it out. Why buy a stock when you know nothing about the company? Becoming educated greatly increases your success. In addition, you have the satisfaction of making your own investment decisions, not relying on someone else.

2. *Invest in a company, not a market.* The Wall Street media has convinced most investors that market conditions are the essential element in the investment equation. While important, the market is only one factor that determines whether a stock's price will go up or down. The main factor affecting the direction of a company's stock movement is the quality of the company itself. If the company has increased its sales and earnings, the stock usually will move upward regardless of the market. However, if the company has experienced huge losses and decreased sales, its stock price normally will drop, even if the market is moving upward. You should spend the majority of your research time analyzing potential investment candidates. The market will take care of itself.

3. *Don't be a jack-of-all-trades and a master of none – specialize in one area.* Learning everything about all types of investments is overwhelming and a waste of time. One way to reduce this to a more manageable load is to specialize in one area of investing. Becoming an educated investor in a specific area can prove extremely lucrative. My research shows that investors can far outpace the market by specializing in quality, low-priced stocks, an area generally ignored by mainstream Wall Street.

4. *Don't fall victim to the greed/fear trap.* A pitfall that catches most investors at one time or another is the greed/fear trap. Greed enters into the picture when an investor has made a nice profit on a stock, but hesitates to take it, believing that it will continue to rise. When the stock price starts to fall, the investor becomes afraid to sell, because he assumes it will go up again. Instead he does nothing,

and watches as the stock eventually backs down to, or below, the original purchase price.

5. *Avoid high-priced stocks.* When investors purchase higher-priced stocks, they encounter two obstacles to successful investing. The first is that many higher-priced stocks are so expensive that it is almost impossible for them to double in price. Those stocks have already experienced their major growth. Secondly, the investor has no leverage, since it takes more capital than the average investor would have, to purchase a large block of shares. Anyone can buy a $50 per share blue chip stock. The challenge is to find a good stock under $5, which has the potential to go to $50. As unlikely as this seems, some of the stocks that I have recommended in my newsletter have done just that!

6. *Controlling larger amounts of shares will translate into higher profits.* Your money goes much farther with low-priced stocks. You can buy a lot more shares for the same amount of money. For example – with $5,000 you can buy 100 shares of a $50 stock, or 5,000 shares of a $1 stock. If both go up $1, the $50 stock will realize a $100 profit, while the $1 stock will experience a $5,000 profit. Controlling a large amount of shares is truly one of the secrets of getting rich.

7. *Always look at profits and losses in percentages, not in dollars and cents.* Successful investors look at profits and losses with a different perspective. Instead of viewing price movements in points ($1 is referred to as one point and $1.50 would be 1.5 points), smart investors convert the price movement into a percentage. How would you have profited if the $50 stock went up $10 and the $1 stock rose only $0.50? Offhand, you may say the $50 stock performed better. However, if you figure the profit percentage, you would see that the $50 stock moved up 20 percent while the $1 stock rose 50 percent!

8. *Buying a stock near its low price is key to your profit.* A stock's purchase price becomes the base from which you calculate profit. Most stocks are cyclical. That means that they rise to near their 52-week high, then fall to the low, and move up again. If you buy a stock near its 52-week high, the law of averages is against you. It is smarter to buy a quality stock near its 52-week low, where it has greater profit potential. The simple concept behind making a profit is to buy low and sell high.

9. *Patience can pay off profitably.* It takes patience to wait for a stock to dip near its 52-week low price, but this can mean the difference between a profit and a loss. Many times I have followed a stock for a year or more, before it achieved the perfect combination of being

a high-quality company at a low price. Patience is also important when the stock price languishes at the same level for months on end, or falls at the end of the year due to tax selling. If the company is still in good shape, the patient investor will hold the stock for a long-term profit.

10. *Buy your stock when no one wants it, and sell it when everyone wants to buy.* Every time you buy stock, you are purchasing from shareholders who sold because they think the stock is going down. If you invest contrary to the masses, you can buy the stock while there is little demand for it, and the price is low. Likewise, when other investors are clamoring to buy the stock, and its price goes up, you already will have made a nice profit. That means you can sell and take your profit, while others are just getting into that stock at a much higher price.

11. *Never sell a stock in December just to take a tax loss.* At the end of each year, many brokers, accountants and financial planners recommend that their clients check their portfolios to determine whether they have any stocks that are in a paper-loss position. (The stock's current price is lower than the price at which the stock was purchased.) If so, they advise their clients to sell the stock, and take the loss for tax purposes. I disagree with the timing of this strategy. Statistics show that most low-priced stocks are closer to their 52-week low price in November and December (probably due to other investors selling for a tax loss and driving down the price). Because the investor can sell for a tax loss at any time during the year, he would be much wiser to hold the quality stock, and sell it after it recovers in the first months of the new year.

12. *Don't take anyone else's word; investigate before you invest.* This adage is especially true since the advent of the Internet. Investors are deluged with stock tips from chat lines, unsolicited e-mail newsletters, friends and brokers. Many times an investor is so blinded by greed, that he forgets to ask any questions about the investment. Letting someone else make your investment decisions certainly is easier, yet it makes you more susceptible to high-pressure scam artists. Telephone scam artists pressure you to buy right away, without thinking it over. Never buy an investment without checking it out yourself. There are several Internet stock quote Websites that give a tremendous amount of information about each company, including news releases, and the 10-K and 10-Q reports filed with the Securities and Exchange Commission (SEC). If you can't find any information on the company, don't invest in it. Taking the time to investigate a stock before investing can save you a lot of money and trouble.

13. *Follow your stock price so you don't miss major profit opportunities.* Many investors become lazy after they purchase a stock and don't follow its price. That laziness can be their downfall. Some stocks are very volatile and may double in price, only to fall back a week or two later. If the investor hasn't been watching the price, he may miss a great opportunity to sell their stock for a good profit.

Perhaps the biggest eye opener for me was discovering that I could make more profitable investments by choosing stocks myself rather than relying on someone else. To maintain my success, I realized that I had to learn as much as possible about the stock to intelligently decide whether or not it was a good investment.

•   Rule 1   •

An educated investor is a successful investor

Whenever your broker, friend or relative gives you a stock tip, don't buy the stock without checking its fundamentals. Take the time to learn about the current stock price. Is it selling near the stock's 52-week high or low?

The cardinal rule of investing is to buy a stock at a low price and sell it for a higher price. If the stock you are interested in is already at its historical high, your chances of making a profit are greatly reduced, so stay away from it. If the stock is near its 52-week low price, it may be a good candidate. The next step is to obtain financial information from the company, or on the Internet, and carefully analyze the company's profit potential.

Many people fail to perform this step. Why do intelligent people, who would never consider buying a car without checking to see if it is a good purchase, blindly invest thousands of dollars in companies that basically have nothing to offer? I believe that the overwhelming number of companies and types of investments intimidate most investors. They figure that they can never learn enough, and thus must rely on experts. This is okay as long as the expert knows what he is doing. But if they don't, the investor usually finds out only after the loss of several thousand dollars.

Figure 1.1　　　**Typical Stock Listing in a newspaper**

| 52 Week | | Stock | | | Yield | P/E | Sales | | | | Net |
High	Low	Stock	Symbol	Div.	%	Ratio	100s	High	Low	Close	Change
8.50	3.45	BAIRNCO	BZ	.20	5	6	600	4.63	3.85	4	+.25
(A)		(B)	(C)	(D)	(E)	(F)	(G)	(H)	(1)	(J)	(K)

(A)	52-Week high/low	This is the highest and lowest price per share (high is $8.50 per share, low is $3.45 per share) that this stock traded for during the past 52 weeks.
(B)	Stock	This refers to the name of the stock. In this case it is Bairnco Corporation.
(C)	Stock Symbol	This is the group of letters assigned to a stock so that a broker can access the stock on his computer to check the price and other information.
(D)	*Div.*	The annual cash dividend paid on the stock. Bairnco paid $.20 per share.
(E)	*Yield %.*	The dividend in terms of yield percent. Because there is a $.20 dividend and the close of the stock is $4, the yield percent is 5.
(F)	*P/E ratio*	The price-earnings (P/E) ratio for this stock is 6. The previous day's closing price divided by the latest 12-month per share earnings for the company becomes the P/E ratio. This is used to measure comparative values among different stocks. If there is no P/E ratio, the company is not making money; if there is a P/E ratio, the company is profitable.
(G)	*Sales (100s)*	Refers to the day's trading volume for this stock. The number 600 is in hundreds of shares. Therefore, a total of 60,000 shares traded that day. (You must have both a buy and a sell transaction to constitute a trade.)
(H)	*High*	This is the highest price ($4.63 per share) at which the stock was traded during the day.
(I)	*Low*	This is the lowest price ($3.85 per share) at which the stock was traded during the day.
(J)	*Close*	When the stock exchange bell rings and the market is closed, the last or *closing* price ($4 per share) for which the stock was traded.
(K)	*Net Change*	The difference between today's and yesterday's closing price. In this example, Bairnco was up $.25 per share when compared to the previous day's closing price.

WELCOME TO THE WORLD OF CHEAP INVESTMENTS

One of the basics of investing is following the company's stock price. Some stocks don't move very much, and you may check them only once a week. However, it is a good idea to follow most stocks daily. Sometimes fantastic news can cause a stock price to rise or fall quickly. If you aren't watching, you may miss a profit opportunity.

You can easily check many stocks' prices on the Internet or in *The Wall Street Journal, Investor's Business Daily* and even major local newspapers. When you follow your stock in the newspaper, you'll see several columns. While the meanings of some columns are obvious, others may be confusing. Figure 1.1 shows the various column headings and what they indicate.

THERE IS A BIG DIFFERENCE
BETWEEN A STOCK AND THE MARKET

While the market is one factor that may help a stock's price move up or down, there are other, more important, factors that have greater impact on a stock's price. Those factors include revenues and earnings, growth, products or services, an intriguing story, or even the popularity of the company's industry. As you look for a stock to buy, remember that your main concern is whether the company is a good investment, not if the market will go up or down.

Whenever you read about market volatility, or when you hear a newsperson on television solemnly reading, "The market is down 40 points", have you ever wondered what that means? In most cases, the newsperson is referring to the oldest index, the Dow Jones Industrial Average (DJIA or Dow). The Dow is a price-weighted average of 30 popular blue chip stocks. While those stocks may have averaged an upward or downward movement, the stocks that you own may have remained unchanged, or even moved in the opposite direction.

• Rule 2 •
Invest in a Company, NOT a Market

Two other major indexes are the *NASDAQ Composite* and the *Standard & Poor's 500*. The NASDAQ Composite is the average of the closing prices for all NASDAQ National Market System and all other NASDAQ domestic common stocks. It is a good comparative index for investors whose portfolios contain primarily NASDAQ stocks. The Standard & Poor's 500 is comprised of 400 of the largest industrial stocks, 60 transportation and utility stocks, and 40 financial stocks. The index is good for investors who own primarily mutual funds.

Too many investors waste precious time worrying about what the market is going to do rather than devoting that time to finding a stock with good profit potential. Following the market is a dangerous game, because by reacting to the market movement, instead of acting on information, the investor is always one step behind. This means that they will just be getting into a stock when its price is high instead of being able to take a nice profit because they bought when the price was low.

To put this into perspective, let's look back to March 2000 when the NASDAQ Index hit an all-time high of 5,132. Those were exciting times.

Investors' stock values skyrocketed, and many were convinced that they would retire rich on their profits. The record-breaking amount of money being invested in the market helped fuel the boom. The NASDAQ was trading over 2.2 billion shares daily. Then the bubble burst. It's been three years since that market high, and Hollywood couldn't have written a sadder script. By March 2003, NASDAQ's value plunged 75 percent, trading volume fell 50 percent to 1.1 billion daily, and the amount of money trading each day plummeted 90 percent. This is when the smart investor, not the market follower, will be buying good stocks at low prices.

Even though we had a severely depressed market, there were many stocks that were going up. Despite the weak market at the end of 2002, several of my recommendations hit new highs during that year. They included Argosy Gaming, CarMax, Bradley Pharmaceuticals, PetSmart, Neoware and Cache.

Stock	Recommended Price	High Price	Percent Change
Argosy Gaming (AGY)	2.25	41.50	1,744%
CarMax, Inc. (KMX)	1.56	34.00	2,079%
Bradley Pharmaceuticals (BPRX)	1.25	24.00	1,820%
PetSmart Inc. (PETM)	2.50	21.00	740%
Neoware Systems, Inc. (NWRE)	1.56	19.50	1,150%
Cache, Inc. (CACH)	3.22	18.45	473%

These stocks are great examples of good quality, low-priced companies that performed well during a plunging market. They are consumer-oriented companies and, interestingly, they performed better during the bear market.

In a bear market, the stock movements tend to be much smaller. For the past few years, many stocks have experienced these smaller and more frequent price swings. In this type of market, if you have a stock that has risen 30, 40 or 50 percent, you should consider taking at least part of your profit before the price moves down again, and you have lost the opportunity. As you can see, trading quality, low-priced stocks is a good method for making money in a volatile market.

What should you do, if you sold your stock for a profit and it continues to rise? Don't buy that stock at the much higher price, hoping it will continue to go higher. That is a great way to lose money. Instead, you should be following several other investment candidates. You can invest your capital in one of the other stocks that are at a good low price. By studying this book you can learn how to best make a profit from CHEAP stocks.

Chapter

2

Common Stocks are
Your BEST Investment

By purchasing stocks, investors are sharing in the growth of the free enterprise system. This opportunity is available to everyone. No wonder more and more people are taking advantage of it and investing in common stocks. Since interest rates have plunged the past few years, more people are purchasing stocks to obtain higher rates of return than are available in other investment vehicles. This chapter will help you understand what common stocks are, and why you should invest in them.

Even if you have never called a broker and bought a common stock, you already may be investing in them through your pension fund, profit-sharing plan or mutual fund. The major attraction of common stocks is that over the long run, they outperform all other investments. They are easy to buy and sell, fairly simple to research and, most important of all, volatile with the potential for producing excellent profits.

The first three years of the new millennium were tough. In fact the NASDAQ Index fell 39 percent in 2000, 21 percent in 2001 and 31 percent in 2002. Many investors who lost money in the recent bull market have sought new types of investments. Look in any financial section in a bookstore and you'll see many "Get Rich Quick" books. Most of them claim that if you just follow their secret strategy, you too can be rich.

This book is different, because first of all, I don't have a "secret" strategy. I adapted the time-tested, blue chip philosophy of finding companies with good fundamentals (increasing sales and earnings), and then added the key ingredient, of buying that stock when it's selling at, or near, its 52-week low. That's my "secret", buying low and selling high. I specialize in stocks under $5, look for the bargains, and then bet on the growth of our economic system to take the price higher where I sell for a nice profit. Ever since I started writing *The CHEAP Investor* newsletter in 1981, this investment philosophy has worked extremely well for my subscribers in both good and bad markets.

WHAT IS A COMMON STOCK?

When you purchase common stock, you become a part owner of the company. The number of shares you buy determines your percentage of ownership in the firm. As a common-stock owner, you can share in the future of the company's earnings as well as vote (one vote per share) on major issues affecting the company, such as a merger, buyout offer or acquisition. The ownership of common stock gives the investor a way of participating in the growth of virtually any public corporation. In addition, owning common stock helps protect the investor against inflation, since over the years, common stocks have far outpaced inflation.

Because thousands of companies offer shares of common stock, the investor has the opportunity to invest in a broad spectrum of industries. With virtually any investment, you face the danger of some financial loss. However, by investing in quality, low priced stocks and diversifying your investments, you can greatly reduce your risk and still increase your profit potential.

There are two basic ways to make money from common stock: (1) dividends or (2) appreciation (from the sale of the stock after it increases from your purchase price). Very few low-priced stocks pay dividends; however, the growth potential of a bargain stock bought at a low price far outweighs any dividend. There are several catalysts that can cause a stock's price to rise:

- The company has increased its sales and profits.
- The company's industry is experiencing a boom period that may favorably affect the stock's price.
- The company has announced a new product, acquisition or large sales contract.
- The company is approached for a merger or takeover (or there are rumors that this will be attempted).
- A major Wall Street brokerage firm recommends buying the stock.

Of course, sometimes the company announces tremendous news, and the stock price stays the same or goes down. Likewise, the company may have poor earnings, bad management, or announce negative news, yet the stock price goes up. The stock price reaction is not always rational, and that's what can make investing risky. A good bull market will push the price of most stocks in a particular industry upward, whether they deserve the higher price or not. We saw this phenomenon a lot in the late 90s. Conversely, during the first three years of the new century, we saw how a bear market can take a stock's price down, even though the company is in excellent shape.

TYPES OF COMMON STOCKS

Common stocks can be divided into several different categories of stocks. Sometimes a stock may fall into more than one category; for example, a company may be considered both a blue chip and an income stock.

Blue Chip Stocks

Blue chips are widely known companies with long histories of earnings and dividends. Wall Street promotes blue chips as long-term, "safe" investments, which, presumably, offer a low-risk potential and provide a modest return. IBM, General Motors, General Electric and the other well known stocks, listed on the Dow Jones indexes are considered blue chip stocks.

The problem with blue chip stocks is that they typically are extremely high priced ($40 and up), and the small investor can purchase only a few shares. Blue chips are huge, established companies that have already experienced a major period of growth. In my opinion, they usually offer the investor a small return on an overpriced stock. Blue chip stocks are generally listed on the New York Stock Exchange (NYSE), and most of the time they follow the market on its upward and downward swings. However, because their stock prices are so high, blue chip stocks generally do not move over 50 percent in a year.

Growth Stocks

Although they are less well known than blue chips, growth stocks still receive a good amount of publicity. They have enjoyed a history of increasing sales and earnings for several years, and are promoted by Wall Street as good investments in a bull market. Because they are younger (10 to 25 years old) and smaller than the blue chip companies, they offer greater growth potential, they also usually grow faster than the economy and other companies in their industry. If a growth stock gives any dividend, it is very small. Motorola, Microsoft, Wal-Mart, Amgen and Intel are examples of growth stocks.

Growth stocks normally range in price from $20 to $55, which means that the small investor again can afford only a few shares. They usually grow at higher percentages than blue chip stocks, but they rely heavily on the health of the economy and their industry for that growth.

Income Stocks

These well-established companies have existed for a long time. They experience very small growth, normally about the same as the Gross Domestic Product (GDP). However, the company returns most of its profits to the shareholder in the form of dividends. Income stocks tend to be high priced, and Wall Street sells them as very "safe" investments. In many cases the investor receives a dividend that barely covers inflation. AT&T, Commonwealth Edison, other telecom and utility stocks are regarded as income stocks and are not suited to an investor looking for growth. These "safe" investments got hammered, along with the rest of the market from 2000 to 2003. AT&T fell from $60 to $5 and executed a 1 for 5 reverse stock split in order to get its price up to the $25 level. Investors who, a few years ago, bought AT&T for the dividends aren't very happy right now.

Fad Stocks

Fad stocks are usually created by Wall Street analysts in an industry that expands at a much greater rate than the Gross Domestic Product (GDP). A fad stock's price typically flies upward as investors jump on the bandwagon to buy. Because its price moves up so fast, the fad stock comes to the attention of more and more investors, and they buy at higher and higher prices. Unfortunately, the fad stock's price quickly becomes extremely over inflated, when compared to the company's true worth.

Many investors lose money in fad stocks because they buy the stock when it is receiving a lot of publicity and the stock price is already high. Common sense eventually prevails, and the stock's price starts to fall (usually after the small investor has just bought it at record high prices). If the investor does not sell quickly, he may end up with a large loss as the stock gravitates toward a lower and more reasonable price.

Companies in the high-technology and medical industries are prone to fads, especially companies researching cures for major diseases such as cancer or AIDS. Even the rumor that a company may have a treatment for such life-threatening diseases can cause the stock to skyrocket.

A great example of fad stocks, are the Internet stocks that soared to unbelievable highs in the late 1990s. I recommended one company, Hauppauge Digital (NASDAQ – HAUP) at $2.81. The company, which was involved in wireless Internet, soared to a high of $96 or +3,316 percent!   Once the Internet bubble burst, Hauppauge and all the other Internet stocks plunged.   By December 2002, I again recommended it at $1.18.

Figure 2.1 Fonar's Trading Cycles

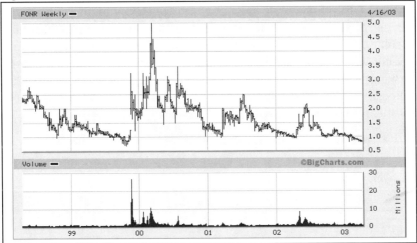

Occasionally a fad stock has real sales and earnings, and after it runs with the fad, it becomes a growth stock.   Argosy Gaming (NYSE – AGY) is an example.   The company owns and operates several gambling riverboats and related entertainment facilities in the Midwest and Southern United States.   When gambling stocks became hot in the late 90s, the stock soared from my buy recommendation at $2.25 in January 1999 to a high of $41.50 in 2002 or +1,744 percent!   The stock price has since fallen back, but still is over $20 per share.

The investors who made truly great profits bought when the stock was low, before it became a fad.   They didn't follow the crowd that bought the stock at higher and higher prices.   Instead, they sold for tremendous profits when everyone else was buying and driving the price upward.

Cyclical Stocks

As the name implies, cyclical stocks move up and down in a price cycle.   Investors can make some good profits by taking advantage of the stock's price cycle and buying near the low.   In general, small cyclical stocks tend to move between 50 to 200 percent through the cycle.   For example, I recommended Fonar each time it was $1 or below, and investors who bought at that price had the potential to make profits of 100 percent or more each year.   Its weekly fluctuations can be seen in figure 2.1.

One strategy that has worked well for my subscribers is to take some of the profits when the stock reaches the high point of the cycle, but to hold on to some shares. I've seen several instances where Wall Street "discovers" the stock and the price skyrockets. For example, Bradley Pharmaceuticals (NYSE – BDY) cycled between $1 and $2 for a number of years. Then Wall Street found the stock and it soared to $32.50 for at least a 1,575 percent increase!

Almost all stocks experience a price cycle to some degree. Blue chips and income stocks may not show a great variation between the low and high price, while some quality, low-priced stocks may experience huge price swings one or more times a year. Properly analyzing a stock to determine its quality and taking advantage of its price cycles can create high profits for the investor.

Figure 2.2 Market Capitalization Categories

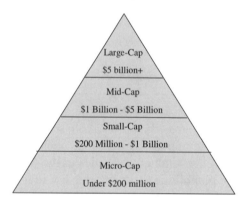

Large-Cap, Mid-Cap, Small-Cap and Micro-Cap Stocks

With the tremendous growth of Mutual Funds in the past decade, Wall Street has started to categorize stocks according to their market capitalization. Market capitalization (market cap) is determined by multiplying a company's number of outstanding shares by its current market price. For example, if Wal-Mart has 4.4 billion shares outstanding and is currently selling at $50 per share, it has a market capitalization of $220 billion (4.4 billion x $50). Wall Street has created four distinct groups as shown in figure 2.2.

Large-Cap Stocks have a market cap in excess of $5 billion. These stocks are generally the oldest, most well known companies that have a long history of established products and profitability. This segment has the smallest number of companies, but the largest number of analysts follow these stocks. Generally, the stock price is very high and the growth potential is low. Low risk is the selling point for this group. The bear market in the first three years of the new millennium hammered these stocks with the rest of the market. Personally, I think these stocks are one of the worst buys for the small investor.

Mid-Cap Stocks normally have a market cap between $1 and $5 billion. More companies fall into this sector than the Large-Cap Stocks. The number of analysts who follow these stocks is still large. Mid-Cap Stocks have a short history of good growth in revenues and earnings, and most companies are in high-growth technical industries. The stocks normally outperform a bull market but plunge along with the rest of the stocks in a bear market. Unfortunately, the majority of stocks in this category are overpriced which is a major stumbling block when looking for high profit potential.

Small-Cap Stocks generally have a market capitalization between $200 million and $1 billion. Even fewer analysts follow the large number of stocks that compose this sector. Many of the companies in this group are young and still have a lot of room for growth. Stock prices are normally higher than Micro-Caps and can be a good investment if the company has good increasing sales and earnings, and the stock is selling near its 52-week low price.

Micro-Cap Stocks are the "cheapies" of the industry. The largest portion of companies fall into this group, which is defined as having under a $200 million market capitalization. Ironically, this huge group of companies has only a small following of analysts. Many shortsighted people automatically write off the Micro-Caps as too risky. Granted the companies are very young, perhaps 5 to 10 years old. Traditionally, the stock prices are the lowest in this group, usually under $5 per share.

I concentrate on this group of ignored stocks, because I believe they have the greatest profit potential for individual investors. Within this group, there are several subgroups, but the two that I like to follow are turnarounds and unknowns. Many turnaround companies were formerly Mid- or Small-Cap stocks that fell on hard times. As the stock price plunged, the market capitalization shrank until it fell to the Micro-Cap category. In the interim, the company's management instituted changes that helped to turn around its sales and earnings. Usually the stock is very undervalued and a great bargain for the wise investor who realizes its true worth.

Unknown stocks are the companies that analysts don't follow. The company has a boring product and no attention-grabbing story to excite investor interest. However, getting positioned in a boring, unknown stock can reap tremendous profits for the patient investor.

Time and again I have seen Micro-Cap stocks make amazing moves. I think these stocks have the greatest profit potential of all, if the investor buys a quality company at a good low price.

COMMON STOCKS OFFER EXCELLENT LIQUIDITY

What is liquidity? Liquidity is the ability to convert assets into cash during a short period of time. This should be a major consideration in every investment you make. Anyone who has sold a home is familiar with liquidity. Everyone has heard horror stories where a homeowner waited months or, in extreme cases years, between the time the house was offered for sale and when it was sold. While professional appraisers can estimate an appropriate price, in the end, a house is worth only what someone else is willing to pay for it.

Investors in collectibles such as coins, stamps, dolls, beanie babies, collectors' plates, etc., often find that when they want to sell, the market is small. Even though a plate, coin or other collectible may be worth a certain amount according to magazine articles, in many cases, no one offers anything close to that amount.

A friend of mine decided to invest in collectors' plates after reading about the amazing profits she could make. One company claimed the distinction of being a collectors' plate exchange and compared itself to a stock exchange. Supposedly, she could buy plates from the company, and when the price went up, she could sell her plates on the exchange.

This sounded like a good opportunity, so my friend decided to invest. A Norman Rockwell plate appreciated from her $17 purchase price to a value of $160 according to literature she received from the exchange. She had purchased ten plates, so she figured her $170 investment was now worth $1,600 for an 841 percent profit in just two years! When she called the exchange to sell her plates, they confirmed the $160 value but recommended that she discount it by 25 percent so the plates would sell faster. There also was a 20 percent commission when the exchange sold her plates. That would net her $96 per plate. This was quite a bit below the $160 value but still not bad.

However, after several months the plates hadn't sold, and when she called the exchange, they suggested she again lower her price. She did – first to $75, then to $50 and finally to $35. In desperation, she visited stores that sold collectors' plates and finally was able to sell six for $192 or $32 each. She never did sell any plates through the exchange. She now keeps one plate hanging above her desk to remind her of that investment. Since then, she has invested only in common stocks because she knows that they offer greater liquidity, and that it will be easier to find a buyer when she wants to sell.

Common stocks that are traded on the NYSE, the Amex or the NASDAQ can quickly be bought or sold for specifically quoted prices. You can call your broker, ask for the latest trade price for the stock and then instruct him to buy or sell either for a specific price or at the market price (i.e., the best price available at the time the order is executed). Your broker can buy or sell your stock at the market price in a matter of seconds. The great liquidity of common stocks, compared with many other long-term investments, is a tremendous advantage, and a major reason why common stocks are the most popular investment.

COMMON STOCKS POSSESS GREAT PROFIT POTENTIAL

Numerous types of investments are available. To mention a few, you can buy real estate, rare coins, diamonds, stamps, gold, silver and other precious metals, rare books, futures, commodities, tax shelters, art, antiquities or options.

Many investors have tried one or more of these investments with varying degrees of success. In fact, after the 1987 market crash, many investors became disillusioned with common stocks, for they believed that stocks were too speculative. They decided to put their money in "safer" investments, such as real estate, options, commodities or futures.

Because they knew nothing about these investments, some became easy marks for scam artists. Others lost money because they weren't knowledgeable enough to make wise investment decisions. They discovered that the people who really make good profits investing in art, coins, diamonds and other collectibles are experts who are educated to recognize a bargain. In order to be this expert, most of them specialize in a specific collectible.

Those who turned to other types of investments after that crash, eventually learned the folly of that decision when they missed the greatest bull market in our history during the 1990s.

1990s Bull Market

Index	Year Index Established	10-Year Gain in 1990s
DJIA	1896	270%
NASDAQ Composite	1971	750%
NYSE Composite	1966	235%
Russell 2000	1984	210%
S&P 500	1957	305%

Even though the crash of 1987 was a long time ago, investors learned an extremely important lesson. Unlike the majority who sold after the crash, smart investors bought extremely undervalued stocks, patiently held on to them, and eventually wound up with huge profits.

Common stocks are an investment for all times. They represent the best investment for the vast majority of individuals. They are attractive because, over the long haul, common stocks produce better results than most other investments. They have a ready marketplace for both buying and selling. Common stocks are more appropriate and more affordable for the small investor, who may not have much money to invest.

Of course, to make intelligent investment decisions, the investor must be willing to spend some time and effort learning about common stocks. Successful common stock investing involves using all that knowledge when researching potential investments to select the best stock match for your goals. My objective is to show you the path to becoming the best possible investor.

RISK VERSUS PROFIT POTENTIAL

While all investments have a degree of risk, certain types are normally less dangerous than others. When you contemplate your choice, consider your risk versus your profit potential. Figure 2.3 shows several types of investments and their degree of risk.

Ironically, because the small investor does not have much money to invest, he must make the best profit possible. A large investor who has $1,000,000 can afford to invest in U.S. securities, such as ten-year Treasury bonds at 4 percent. However, a small investor with only $1,000 or $2,000 in capital needs a higher profit rate, or his money may never amount to much.

Figure 2.3 Risk versus Profit Potential

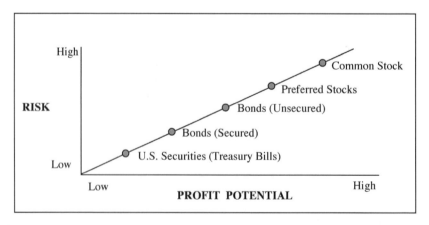

After the market meltdown in 2000, investors left the market in droves, just as they did after the 1987 crash. Many of those investors are still looking for a "safe" investment. With interest rates at a 40-year low, safe investments, like Treasury Bills, are paying extremely low interest rates. Currently the rate is only about 3 percent. The chart below shows how a $1,000 investment increases over the years.

Figure 2.4   Three Percent Growth for $1,000

Year	Amount
1	$1,030
5	1,126
10	1,305
20	1,754
25	2,033

As you can see, your $1,000 grows very slowly at that low rate. In fact, it takes 25 years to double your money. The investment may be safe, but the return may not even keep up with inflation. In addition, the investor has to pay taxes on the profits. I think there is a better way to invest. History shows that investing in common stocks over a long period of time is the best single investment for individual investors. Over the years, common stocks have far outpaced inflation.

COMMON STOCKS AND YOUR TAXES

Each time you buy or sell a stock, your brokerage firm will send a trade confirmation that details the price you paid or received for your shares, the number of shares traded and the commission fee. The brokerage firm will also send a copy of the confirmation to the Internal Revenue Service (IRS). At the beginning of each year your brokerage firm will send you a form 1099-B for the previous year that details your buy and sell transactions and any interest you made or dividends you received from your investments. It's a good idea to keep all your stock trade confirmation forms. They can help you check that 1099-B form for accuracy when you file your taxes.

Note: When listing your stock transactions on tax form Schedule D, remember to add your commission when you buy, and subtract your commission when you sell. Commission fees are not a part of your profits. Also, check with your tax adviser about whether you can deduct the cost of this book and subscriptions to financial newsletters and newspapers.

Capital Gains

The 1997 Taxpayer Relief Act unveiled a new capital gains tax schedule with most rates reduced. There are two holding periods for capital assets sold:

- Those held for one year or less are considered short-term and receive no preferred tax treatment. You pay taxes at your "normal" tax rate on those gains.

- Those held for more than one year are considered long-term and you receive a tax break on the sale of those assets – currently the rate is set at 20 percent.

Make sure you plan for your taxes. Many investors don't put aside enough money and wind up in trouble when taxes are due. It's interesting to note that when capital gains taxes are reduced, the stock market usually soars. This occurred when capital gains were cut in 1964 under President Kennedy and in 1981 under President Reagan. Most recently, the stock market hit new highs between 1998 and March 2000 after the 1997 Taxpayer Relief Act took effect.

By the way, the United States is the only industrialized country in the world that taxes profits from stock investments. Perhaps those foreign investors who buy U.S. stocks have the funds to do so because they don't have to pay capital gains taxes.

USING YOUR STOCK AS COLLATERAL

At one time or another, everyone has experienced an emergency when they needed cash quickly. If your money is invested in real estate for example, it could take a couple of months to a year before you are able to convert your property into cash. Two major advantages of common stock are that you can sell it at any time and can easily find the current price through Internet quote services.

If Murphy's Law comes into play, the time you need money is also the time when your stock price is depressed. This is one time you may be able to have your cake and eat it too, because sometimes you can use your stock as collateral for a loan. Offering your stock as collateral allows you to borrow the cash you need without having to sell your stock when the price is depressed.

There are two ways to obtain a loan using stock as collateral. You can approach your local bank. Since they already do business with you, they would be more open to offering you 50 to 80 percent of the stock's value. The variation in percentage is caused by differences in banks and the quality of the stock that you're offering as collateral. Be aware that if the stock price falls, your bank will require additional collateral.

The other way to obtain emergency money is very risky, and I don't recommend it. You can open a margin account with your brokerage firm. This will allow you to borrow money from that broker. Before considering this dangerous tactic, be aware that as long as the stock you offer as collateral goes up you are fine. However, if the stock price falls, you will receive a margin call from the broker to deposit enough money or securities to bring your margin account up to the minimum maintenance requirements. If you fail to respond to the margin call, your securities will be liquidated.

Make a pact with yourself to sell the stock and pay off the loan when the stock moves up. Too many investors watch their stock move up and then move back down because they thought it would move higher. If the stock falls too low, a margin call could spell disaster.

Common stocks offer a high profit potential. However, they also present a greater risk factor. By becoming an educated investor and understanding how the common stock market works, analyzing a stock with good potential, purchasing it at the best price and watching for signs indicating that you should take your profit and sell, you can greatly reduce these risks. The majority of the time, if you invest in a high-quality, low-priced stock, your chances of making a profit are excellent.

Chapter

3

Stock Exchanges –
The Foundation of the Market

Webster's defines a stock exchange as an organized marketplace for the buying and selling of securities. Exchanges provide a place for the daily auction activities of trading, while regulating their members. These institutions are the central actors in the drama of the world of common stocks.

From the visitors' gallery, the floor of the New York Stock Exchange looks like a wild mass of confusion, with people shouting, making strange hand gestures and running back and forth. Believe it or not, that "mass of confusion" is actually very organized and conducts the serious business of buying and selling stocks. With a short orientation to the process, all of this confusion settles into a frantic, but ordered choreography of actors, with the exchange as the center stage.

UNDERSTANDING AN EXCHANGE STOCK TRANSACTION

If Sally Jones wants to buy 1,000 shares of Xerox there are several steps involved in the transaction.

- Sally calls her broker and asks him for Xerox's price.
- The broker states that Xerox is trading at $8.63, after consulting his computer, which is connected to an electronic data-market system from the NYSE Trading Floor.

- Sally likes the $8.63 cost and instructs her broker to purchase 1,000 shares at that price.

- The broker sends Sally's order to the Trading Floor post using either the Broker Booth Support System (BBSS) or SuperDot.

- At the post, floor brokers match Sally's buy order with a sell order for 1,000 shares of Xerox. A specialist in Xerox oversees the transaction, to make sure it is executed in a fair and orderly manner.

- After the trade is executed, the specialist's workstation sends notice to the brokerage firm and the consolidated audit tape.

- The transaction is reported by computer and appears within seconds on the consolidated tape displays across the country and around the world.

- Within three days the brokerage firm sends Sally a written confirmation of her purchase of 1,000 shares of Xerox, for $8.63 per share.

- Sally settles her account within three business days by submitting payment to her brokerage firm. (Many discount brokerage firms require that you have enough money in your account to cover the cost of the trade before they will execute it.)

Looking more closely at the different exchanges also adds to the general understanding of the general flow of a stock trade. The view of each exchange includes both history and the listing requirements for the exchange.

NEW YORK STOCK EXCHANGE (NYSE)

Founded in 1792, the NYSE is the largest stock exchange in the United States. It is located at 11 Wall Street in New York City and is known as the "Big Board" and the "Exchange." More than 3,000 of the largest, most well known and profitable U.S. companies are listed on the NYSE.

The NYSE is an incorporated, not-for-profit organization headed by a full-time chairperson and governed by a board of directors. This board represents the public and the exchange membership in about equal proportion. Its functions include membership regulation and surveillance, finance and office services, product development and planning, market servicing and public relations. The NYSE also handles legal problems, government regulations and economic research for member firms.

What makes the NYSE unique? It's like an auction. Each day on the NYSE trading floor open bids and offers are shouted out by Exchange members, acting on behalf of institutions and individual investors. Buy and sell orders for each listed security meet directly on the trading floor in assigned locations. Prices are determined through supply and demand. Stock buy and sell orders funnel through a single location, ensuring that the investor, no matter how big or small, is exposed to a wide range of buyers and sellers.

The total of 1,366 seats on the NYSE allow the owner to be a member and trade on the floor of the exchange. Brokerage firms own most of these seats. Trading is conducted through an advanced centralized system, combining the speed of computer-delivered orders with the liquidity of customer driven markets. Specialists are responsible for maintaining an orderly market in the securities they handle. Most members execute orders for the public, institutions and mutual funds; a few floor traders deal exclusively for their own accounts. Stocks, bonds, warrants, options and rights are all traded on the NYSE.

Listing Requirements for the NYSE

Minimum Standards	Requirements
Shareholders	
Round-lot holders (generally 100 shares)	2,000
Or	
Total shareholders together with	2,200
Average monthly trading volume (last 6 months)	100,000 shares
Or	
Total shareholders together with	500
Average monthly trading volume (last twelve months)	1,000,000 shares
Public Shares	1,100,000
Market Value of public shares	$60,000,000 (IPOs & spinoffs)
	$100,000,000 (all others)
Or	
	$60,000,000 (IPOs & spinoffs)
Equity	$100,000,000 (all others)
Demonstrated earning power over three most recent fiscal years	
Most recent year Pre-tax earnings	$2,500,000
Each of the two preceding years Pre-tax earnings	$2,000,000
Or	
Minimum in the most recent year Pre-tax earnings	$4,500,000
(all three years must be profitable)	

Once a company meets with a listing regional manager, it is asked to send specific information to the exchange, including its past three years of audited balance sheets, Form 10-Ks and annual reports. After reviewing the information, the Listed Company Advisory Committee (LCAC), which includes chief executive officers (CEOs) and presidents of NYSE member companies, interview the company. If the LCAC determines that the company meets the requirements, the company is asked to apply formally for listing on the NYSE. This process normally takes six to ten weeks, from the date of application, to the company's actual listing on the exchange.

Why go through the hassle to become listed? A major advantage of the NYSE listing is the tremendous exposure a company enjoys after joining the almost 3,000 elite companies already on the exchange. Interestingly, the vast majority of major institutional investors buy only stocks that are listed on the NYSE. Another advantage is that it is much easier to raise capital once the company is a member of the NYSE.

The NYSE offers a number of publications of interest to the investor. For further information, contact the Publication Department, New York Stock Exchange (20 Broad St., 24th Floor, New York, NY 10005 or call 212-656-5273). The Internet address is www.nyse.com.

AMERICAN STOCK EXCHANGE (Amex)

The American Stock Exchange (Amex) was formed in the 1840s around the time of the California gold rush. It is the second most well known stock exchange, although it ranks below the National Association of Securities Dealers Automated Quotations (NASDAQ) system in terms of volume and dollar value of trading.

The Amex was known as the Curb Market from 1911 to 1921, because transactions took place on the curb at Trinity Place, in New York City. This is sometimes still referred to as the "Curb." In 1921 it moved indoors to 86 Trinity Place, where it is still located. In 1929, the name was modified to the New York Curb Exchange. Not until 1953 was its name changed to the American Stock Exchange.

The Amex operates in a manner similar to the NYSE. The nation's second largest floor-based exchange, the Amex has a significant presence in common stocks, index shares and equity derivative securities. On the Amex, trading is conducted through an advanced centralized Specialist system, combining the speed of computer-delivered orders with the liquidity of customer-driven markets. Most of the almost 1,000 stocks listed on the Amex today are small- to medium-sized businesses. Many of the larger and well-known companies (such as Armour, Borden, Dow Chemical, DuPont, Goodyear, RCA and Standard Oil of California) traded on the Amex before moving to the NYSE.

In 1998, the NASD (National Association of Securities Dealers, Inc.) and the American Stock Exchange merged. The two markets merged to create a market that combined a central auction Specialist system (Amex) and a multiple Market Maker system (NASDAQ). The Amex continues to operate as a separate market.

An example of the synergies in the NASDAQ-Amex Market Group is the NASDAQ-100 Index Tracking Stock, launched for sale on the Amex in early 1999. A unit investment trust, it tracks closely the price and yield performance of the NASDAQ-100 Index. This proved to be the most successful product launch in Amex history, trading 2.6 million shares on its first day.

Listing Requirements for the Amex

Normally companies must meet the following minimum standards to qualify for listing on the Amex. (The membership requirements for the Amex are significantly lower than those for the NYSE.) A company must have the following:

Guidelines	Regular Requirements	Alternative Requirements
Pretax income (latest fiscal year or 2 of most recent 3 fiscal years)	$750,000	N/A
Market Value of public float	$3,000,000	$15 million
Minimum Share Price	$3	$3
Operating History	N/A	3 years
Stockholders' Equity	$4,000,000	$4,000,000
Public Stockholders	Standard 1: 800 Standard 2: 400 Standard 3: 400	
Public Float (shares not held directly or indirectly by any officer or director of the issuer or by any person who is the beneficial owner of 10 percent or more of the total shares outstanding)	Standard 1: 500,000 Standard 2: 1,000,000 Standard 3: 500,000	
Average Daily Volume	Standard 3: 2,000	

Perhaps the main reason for a stock to move up from the NASDAQ market to the Amex is the increased ease in raising capital. When a stock is listed on the NASDAQ market, it must apply individually to each state in which it wants to sell securities. This is very expensive and time consuming.

Once the company is listed on the Amex, it is automatically free to sell its securities in all 50 states. For more information, contact the American Stock Exchange (86 Trinity Place, New York, NY 10006; 212-306-1000). The Internet address is www.amex.com.

REGIONAL STOCK EXCHANGES

While the term regional stock exchange is sometimes used in a derogatory manner, it accurately describes exchange trading located outside of New York. While regional stock exchanges feature the listings of a few local companies, the bulk of their business is obtained from national markets. During the 1960s, 14 regional exchanges operated in the United States. Since then, the weak have either merged or expired, and only five significant exchanges remain: the Chicago, Pacific, Philadelphia, Boston and Cincinnati stock exchanges.

Trading on these exchanges (except for Cincinnati) is pretty much as I previously described. Stocks with certain local following may be listed exclusively with that regional exchange, but the majority of the exchange's trading volume is derived from transactions of NYSE, Amex and NASDAQ-listed stocks. Because of the Intermarket Trading System, it is as easy to buy AT&T from the Boston or Chicago exchange, as it is from the New York exchange. Stock-price quotes from the regional specialists are as competitive as, and sometimes better than, the New York quotes.

The Chicago Stock Exchange
(CHX; formerly Midwest Stock Exchange)

The Chicago Stock Exchange trades more issues than any other stock exchange in the world - more than 3,500 NYSE, Amex, NASDAQ and CHX-exclusive issues. Founded in 1882, this Exchange grew through the mergers in 1949 and 1959 of several separate exchanges, including the Chicago, St. Louis, Cleveland, Minneapolis-St. Paul and New Orleans exchanges. Located in the heart of Chicago's financial district, it is the most active regional exchange by a considerable margin. For more information, call or write the Chicago Stock Exchange (440 S. LaSalle St., Chicago, IL 60605; 312-663-2222). The Internet address is www.chicagostockex.com.

The Pacific Stock Exchange (PCX)

Founded in 1882, the Pacific Stock Exchange (PCX) was the first exchange in the world to build and operate an electronic trading system. It was also the first exchange to demutualize, establishing PCX Equities, Inc. as a for-profit, corporate subsidiary of the PCX in 1999. More than 1,200 stock options are traded on the PCX.

The PCX is also the regulator of the Archipelago Exchange, a fully electronic market for securities listed on the NYSE, Amex, PCX, and NASDAQ markets. The Archipelago Exchange began trading operations in March 2002, and some say this will be the future of how exchanges will operate.

For more information, call or write the Pacific Stock Exchange (115 Sansone St., San Francisco, CA 94104; 415-393-4000). The Internet address is www.pacificex.com.

The Philadelphia Stock Exchange (PHLX)

Founded in 1790 (two years before the NYSE), the Philadelphia Stock Exchange (PHLX) is the oldest organized stock exchange in the United States. During the years, it has merged with the Baltimore and Washington, D.C. exchanges.

The PHLX developed Sectors Index Options, one of the most significant options success stories on any U.S. exchange in the 1990s. Comprising industry-specific and broad-based indices, these instruments made the PHLX an industry leader in sectors index options trading. In fact, several emerged as industry benchmarks, and they are widely quoted barometers of the activity in key market segments. Similarly, the Gold/Silver Sector, the KBW Bank Sector, the Oil Service Sector, the Semiconductor Sector and TheStreet.com Internet Sector have established themselves as leading industry indicators.

For more information, call or write the Philadelphia Stock Exchange (1900 Market St., Philadelphia, PA 19103; 800-THE-PHLX). The Internet address is www.phlx.com.

The Boston Stock Exchange

Founded in 1834, the Boston Stock Exchange is the third oldest stock exchange in the United States. Originally a market center for New England-based stocks, it remains today "New England's exchange" with strong ties to the region's highly developed financial services industry. The Exchange's primary business is trading approximately 2,000 nationally listed equities. It also trades over 200 high-growth company issues that are solely listed on the BSE.

Since 1990, BSE trading activity has increased more than sevenfold. For more information, call or write the Boston Stock Exchange (100 Franklin St., Boston, MA 02110, 617-235-2000.) The Internet address is www.bostonstock.com.

The Cincinnati Stock Exchange

The Cincinnati Exchange has been around since 1885, when a group of Cincinnati businessmen came together to auction the shares of a handful of local companies. Today the Exchange is headquartered in Chicago's financial district, home to many of its members. It now has a physical trading floor with an electronic network providing the same efficiency and timeliness in quote dissemination, trade execution and trade reporting. In 1976 the CSE undertook one of the most significant innovations in the history of auction exchanges, resulting in the replacement of its centralized physical trading floor with an all-new concept, a geographically-dispersed electronic trading floor. For more information, call or write the Cincinnati Stock Exchange (440 south LaSalle Street, 26th Floor, Chicago, IL 60605, 312-786-8803). The Internet address is www.cincinnatistock.com.

THE NASDAQ MARKET

Until 1971, when the NASDAQ was established, this market was known as the Over-the-Counter Market (OTC). The original market name dates back to the late 1700s, when Wall Street was enjoying its first bull market, and merchants, encouraged by increased activity, kept a small inventory of securities on hand that they sold over the counter along with their other goods.

Unlike the NYSE and Amex, which have physical exchange floors, the NASDAQ consists of thousands of securities houses located in hundreds of cities across the country. A communications network that links the securities houses with each other, handles the securities transactions.

The NASDAQ market as we know it today began February 5, 1971, with the formation of the National Association of Securities Dealers Automated Quotations (NASDAQ) system, which is owned and operated by the NASD. In contrast to traditional floor-based stock markets, NASDAQ has no single specialist through which transactions pass. NASDAQ's market structure allows multiple market participants to trade stock through a sophisticated computer network linking buyers and sellers from around the world. Together, these participants help ensure transparency and liquidity for a company's stock, while maintaining an orderly market and functioning under tight regulatory controls.

The NASDAQ market is comprised of more than 4,000 securities that, for the most part, do not meet the more demanding listing requirements of the NYSE and the Amex. NASDAQ stocks are divided into two groups – SmallCaps and the more elite National Market System.

The NASDAQ has grown dramatically over the past ten years, fueled primarily by tremendous growth in high tech stocks. Many of those stocks are household names, such as Microsoft, Intel, Apple, Staples, Starbucks, Costco, Cisco Systems, Dell Computer, and Novell. Interestingly, they have elected to remain on the NASDAQ even after expanding to the point that they could list on the NYSE. For more information, call or write the NASDAQ (9801 Washingtonian Boulevard, Gaithersburg, MD 20878, 301-978-8026). The Internet address is www.nasdaq.com.

The NASDAQ National Market System

The NASDAQ National Market contains NASDAQ's largest and most actively traded securities. A company must satisfy stringent financial, capitalization, and corporate governance standards to be listed on the National Market System. NASDAQ National Market companies include some of the largest, best known companies in the world. The listing requirements are shown in figure 3.1.

Figure 3.1 Listing Requirements for NASDAQ National Market System

Requirements	Option 1	Option 2	Option 3
Stockholders' Equity	$15 million	$30 million	N/A
Market Capitalization	N/A	N/A	$75 million
Or			
Total Assets			$75 million
			and
Total Revenue			$75 million
Pre-Tax Income (in latest fiscal year or 2 of last 3 fiscal years)	$1 million	N/A	N/A
Public Float (shares not held directly or indirectly by any officer or director of the issuer or by any person who is the beneficial owner of 10% or more of the total shares outstanding)	1.1 million	1.1 million	1.1 million
Market Value of Public Float	$8 million	$18 million	$20 million
Minimum Bid Price	$5	$5	$5
Market Makers	3	3	4
Shareholders (round lot holders)	400	400	400
Operating History	N/A	2 years	N/A
Corporate Governance	Yes	Yes	Yes

The NASDAQ SmallCaps Market

The NASDAQ SmallCaps Market is NASDAQ's market for emerging growth companies. As the smaller capitalization tier of NASDAQ, the financial criteria for listing on this market are somewhat less stringent than on the NASDAQ National Market, though the Corporate Governance standards are now the same. As SmallCaps companies become more established, they often move up to the NASDAQ National Market. The listing requirements for the NASDAQ SmallCaps stocks are shown in figure 3.2.

NASDAQ stocks show two prices – the bid and the asked. The asked is the lowest price the investor can pay to buy the stock. The bid is the highest price, which the investor will receive if he sells the stock. The spread is the difference between the bid and the asked price.

Understanding a NASDAQ Stock Transaction

If an investor wants to buy 1,000 shares of Sun Microsystems (NASDAQ - SUNW) at $3.35 asked, he calls his broker or enters his order on his computer. Either way the order for 1,000 shares is sent to the firm's trading room. There are two basic ways to execute the trade. The vast majority of trades are *Agency trades*. In an agency trade, the buy order is matched with a sell order, and the brokerage firm charges the agreed upon price of $3.35, plus a commission fee ranging from $10 to 4 percent of the trade value. The second type of trade is a *Principal trade*. This occurs when the brokerage firm buys a stock such as Sun Microsystems at $3.15 in the morning, and sells it at $3.35 as its price moves upward. In this rare instance, the sale already includes the commission. Very few transactions today are principal trades, because brokerage firms don't want the risk of buying a stock that goes down, and then having to hold it or sell for a loss.

Figure 3.2 Listing Requirements for NASDAQ SmallCaps

Requirements	Initial Listing
Stockholders' Equity	$5 million
Or	
Market Capitalization	$50 million
Or	
Net Income (in latest fiscal year or two of the last three fiscal years)	$750,000
Public Float (shares not held directly or indirectly by any officer or director of the issuer or by any person who is the beneficial owner of 10% or more of the total shares outstanding)	1 million
Market Value of Public Float	$5 million
Minimum Bid Price	$4
Market Makers	3
Shareholders (round lot holders)	300
Operating History	1 year
Or	
Market Capitalization	$50 million
Corporate Governance	Yes

OTC BULLETIN BOARD

The OTC Bulletin Board is a separate and distinct electronic quotation service owned and operated by NASDAQ. It began operations in June 1990, as part of important market structure reforms to provide transparency in the OTC equities Market. The system was designed to facilitate the widespread publication of quotation and last-sale information.

Since December 1993, firms have been required to report trades in all domestic OTC equity securities through the Automated Confirmation Transaction Service SM(ACTSM) within 90 seconds of the transaction.

In April 1997, the SEC approved the operation of the OTCBB on a permanent basis, with some modifications. In May 1997, Direct Participation Programs (DPPs) became eligible for quotation on the OTCBB. In April 1998, all foreign securities and American Depositary Receipts (ADRs) that were fully registered with the SEC became eligible for the display of real-time quotes, last-sale prices, and volume information on the OTCBB.

In early 1999, the SEC approved the OTCBB Eligibility Rule. Securities not quoted on the OTCBB, as of that date, are required to report their current financial information to the SEC, banking, or insurance regulators in order to meet eligibility requirements.

The OTCBB provides access to more than 3,600 securities and includes more than 300 participating Market Makers. It electronically transmits real-time quote, price, and volume information in domestic securities, foreign securities and ADRs. It also displays indications of interest and prior-day trading activity in DPPs.

In 2003, the OTCBB was to have been phased out and replaced by a new, higher quality market, the BBX (Bulletin Board Exchange). The BBX was to have qualitative listing standards, but no minimum share price, market capitalization, or shareholder equity requirements. In August 2003, NASDAQ decided to discontinue its efforts to create the BBX Exchange. I hope the proposed BBX exchange will become a reality sometime in the future. For more information, call the OTC BB at (301) 978-8263. The Internet address is www.otcbb.com.

OTC PINK SHEETS

If a company doesn't meet even the minimum Bulletin Board requirements, it becomes listed on the OTC pink sheets. Until 2000, this was a daily publication that listed the bid and asked prices, and the market makers. The information was printed on pink paper, which is how this group of stocks originally got its name. Currently there are almost 4,000 securities that trade on the pink sheets.

I recommend avoiding all pink-sheet stocks because they are very thinly traded, which can be an insurmountable obstacle when trying to buy or sell at a decent price. In addition, these stocks are not required to file quarterly or annual reports with the SEC, so it is virtually impossible to obtain adequate information supporting an educated decision on the quality of the stock. While not all pink-sheet stocks are bad investments and a few have become listed on NASDAQ, the vast majority of penny-stock scams and violations involve pink-sheet stocks.

Often a pink-sheet company will claim that it will shortly be listed on NASDAQ. Occasionally, they do become listed. Many times, however, this is just talk. The Internet address is www.pinksheets.com.

STOCK INDEXES AND THEIR MARKET EFFECT

There are other significant components to the stock trading process, which need to be added to the comprehensive guide. One of these is the stock index. A stock index (or average) measures and reports value changes in representative stock groupings. As an investor, you can compare the movement of your stock to a particular index to see if your investment is performing better or worse than the average. For example, if you own a stock on the NYSE, you may want to compare it to the Dow Jones Industrials, which is probably the premier index.

The Dow Jones Industrial Average (DJIA or Dow) is considered the barometer of the stock market. Charles H. Dow, the first editor of *The Wall Street Journal*, created the Dow Jones Average on July 3, 1884; it consisted of 11 stocks – 9 railroad companies and 2 industrial companies.

On March 26, 1896, Dow created his first Dow Jones Industrial Average, which was made up of 12 industrial stocks. In 1928, the average was changed to 30 stocks, and even though the companies composing the average have been changed many times, the number has remained at 30 (see figure 3.3). By the way, the Dow isn't really an "industrial" index any longer, because it contains banks (CitiGroup), restaurants (McDonalds), retailers (Home Depot and Wal-Mart) and pharmaceutical companies (Merck).

Many small investors have been scared by the tremendous volatility of this index. Because so many analysts follow it, indications of either an upward or downward movement can influence investors into continuing the trend – which becomes a self-fulfilling prophecy. If everyone believes the market is in trouble and fails to invest, then the market will be in trouble. I believe that many investors spend too much time worrying about the volatility of the Dow Jones Industrials over the short term. They should be more interested in long-term trends.

After the Dow, the most widely followed composite index is the Standard & Poor's 500 Stock Index (S&P 500). It consists of 500 of the largest publicly traded stocks, primarily blue chips. While the S&P 500 is also a blue chip index like the Dow, it differs because it is weighted for market capitalization. That way, the stock movements of larger companies have a greater impact on the index. The performance of most mutual fund managers and stockbrokers is compared to the S&P 500 rather than the Dow.

Figure 3.3 Companies currently in the Dow Jones Industrials Index

AT&T	*Home Depot*
Alcoa	*Honeywell*
American Express	*IBM*
Altria Group	*Intel*
Boeing	*International Paper*
Caterpillar	*Johnson & Johnson*
CitiGroup	*McDonalds*
Coca Cola	*Merck Co.*
Disney (Walt)	*Microsoft*
DuPont	*3M*
Eastman Kodak	*Morgan (JP)*
ExxonMobile	*Proctor & Gamble*
General Electric	*SBC Communications*
General Motors	*United Technologies*
Hewlett Packard	*Wal-Mart*

The NYSE, Amex and NASDAQ market each have a composite index. The NASDAQ Composite Index is the most frequently quoted market index. It consists of all the stocks listed on the NASDAQ, some 4,000 companies. The NASDAQ Composite is also weighted for market capitalization. Because the performance of a few large cap stocks tend to dominate the index, it is considered tech-heavy, reflecting the performance of the technology sector more than the market as a whole.

I like to follow three indexes that you can find daily in *Investor's Business Daily*, *The Wall Street Journal* and in most major newspapers. The NYSE Advance and Decline Ratio shows the number of stocks up and down on a particular day. The New Highs and Lows Index is printed both daily and weekly. It lists stocks from all three exchanges, and I follow the new lows closely to locate potential turnaround companies. The Price Percentage Movers indicates both the top percent winners and losers. By following this index, you can discover some of the more volatile cyclical stocks.

You may also want to follow the transportation or the utilities averages if you own stocks in those industries. The Dow Jones Transportation Average (DJTA) is an index composed of 20 stocks in the transportation industry, including railway, airline and trucking companies. The Dow Jones Utility Average (DJUA) includes 15 stocks in the public utility industry, such as gas and electric companies.

The stock indexes should be used as a quick overall guide, but investors shouldn't waste too much time worrying about daily market fluctuations. They can spend their time more profitably by researching companies, to determine which stocks have better investment potential.

Chapter

Understanding the Investment Process

The purchase of stock is a two-sided activity, where a company decides to sell part of its ownership, and an investor chooses to purchase that offering. It is important to understand both sides of the transaction. From the company's view, it started because someone needed money for his company and didn't have any other way to raise it. From the investor's perspective, buying a stock and watching your money grow is a thrilling experience, and is the basic reason for investing. Let's look at the reasons why a company decides to offer part of its ownership to the public.

WHY A COMPANY DECIDES TO SELL STOCK

While most companies are started with capital from the founder, his family or friends, there usually comes a time when more capital is needed. Perhaps it is necessary to research a new idea for a product or develop the product so it can be marketed. The company may want to expand its marketing areas or modernize various production and corporate offices into a larger, more efficient facility. Whatever the reason, the company must obtain additional capital to implement the change. Many times banks are hesitant to lend money to a company when it needs capital (a Catch-22 situation), so the company's only alternative may be to sell shares of stock to the public. Buying stock gives the investor a part ownership of the company, and grants the right to some voice in how the company is run.

Before the company makes the decision to offer stock, it must consider the advantages and disadvantages of going public. The advantages include:

- Obtaining needed capital, that can be used in many beneficial ways, including
  - increasing working capital
  - expanding research and development
  - extending the company's marketplace
  - hiring additional employees
  - updating or expanding facilities
  - retiring existing debt
  - providing capital for acquisitions
  - increasing the company's net worth
- Attracting key management or technical people
- Motivating the current work force, through stock-option or profit-sharing programs.
- Gaining prestige with brokers nationwide
- Increasing the company's visibility through public relations press releases sent to national media
- Enhancing the company's relationship with its bankers
- Assigning a value to the company in case it is entertaining the idea of merging or being acquired
- Designating a price for the private shares held by the original owners and management
- Providing a basis for collateral and security for debt or pricing when sold as additional monies are needed in the future
- Expanding the company's borrowing capability and allowing it to obtain favorable credit terms for future borrowing
- Providing the fulfillment of wealth, power and prestige for the founders of the company

The disadvantages of going public are also significant and can be summarized as the following:

- Going public involves a relatively high expenditure of capital with no certain guarantee that enough investors will want to buy the stock to make it valuable. (The average cost of a $25 million public offering on NASDAQ is $2.4 million including $1.8 million in underwriting discounts and commissions.)
- The company will lose privacy. It must make public information about its sales, profits, losses, mode of operation,

competitive position, management's salaries, lawsuits and many other aspects affecting the company.

- Additional costs will be involved to keep the shareholders up to date with annual reports, quarterly reports, press releases, etc. After going public, most companies are required to file quarterly and annual reports (10-Q and 10-K) with the Securities and Exchange Commission. Legal costs usually skyrocket because of the need for additional legal expertise to write the regulatory reports. Typical expenses for reports can run more than $100,000 a year.

- The company's management loses some of its decision-making control to the shareholders for major decisions, such as conducting a merger or changing its name.

- More pressure is exerted on the company to show increased sales and earnings each year.

Going public is an important decision for a company to make. In many cases, if the company wants to continue to grow, going public may be the only logical choice. This works to the advantage of investors, for it gives them the opportunity to invest in some great companies.

SPECIALIZING IN ONE AREA RATHER THAN IN MANY

One of the biggest mistakes an investor can make is spending too much time looking at too many different types of investments. The investor ends up spreading himself too thinly and learns a little about a lot and not a lot about anything. The average investor has only so much time to devote to developing an understanding of investments. To be a more efficient investor, your time is better spent by specializing in a particular type of investment that interests you.

Once you start researching a certain type of investment, you begin to realize just how much you don't know. This can be overwhelming. There is much to assimilate, such as how the investment works, why it goes up and down in value, how to research that investment, what criteria point to a more potentially successful investment and what is the best way to make money in that investment. It takes a long time to master just one area of investments. I learned that years ago and devoted my time to stocks under $5 per share. I believe that specializing in an area I understand has been a major contribution to the success of my newsletter, *The CHEAP Investor*.

```
•          Rule 3          •

Don't be a jack-of-all trades and a master of none –
                specialize in one area
```

You can choose many different ways to specialize. For example, you can restrict your investigations to a certain type of investment, such as common stocks, options, futures or mutual funds. This book is limited to common stocks. However, approximately 60,000 common stocks are listed on the NYSE, Amex, NASDAQ, OTC Bulletin Board (BB), pink sheets and foreign exchanges.

I decided to focus on stocks under $5 listed on the NYSE, Amex, NASDAQ and OTC BB, which reduced the number to under 5,000 stocks. Then I specialized further by looking only at quality stocks (those of profitable, established companies), which narrowed the base to less than 1,000 stocks, a more manageable number.

If you think that is still too many stocks, you may want to restrict your research to certain industries, specific prices or particular exchanges. This will reduce the number of companies to an amount that you can comfortably investigate.

Spending your time researching various companies in the area in which you specialize can be extremely profitable. Focusing your attention on a much smaller area may allow you to surprise your friends and yourself with the competent opinions you are able to voice on those stocks. (Your opinion, if well researched, may be more knowledgeable than that of many "experts.")

THE GREED/FEAR TRAP

During the bull market of the late 1990s, we witnessed some tremendous increases in stock prices. Many investors saw their stocks move up quickly and continued to watch as the prices fell back to or below their original purchase point. Those investors had fantastic paper profits, but they didn't take them. When the stock prices started to fall, they assumed the prices would rise again. Instead, the investors' paper profits disappeared, and they lost their opportunity to take some very nice profits.

What happened? I call it the greed/fear trap. Here is what happens. The investor buys a quality, low-priced stock at $1 per share. The stock price starts to rise, hitting $2, $3, $4, $5, and up to a high of $5.75. The investor now has a tremendous profit and decides to sell when the stock hits $6.

Figure 4.1 The Greed/Fear Trap

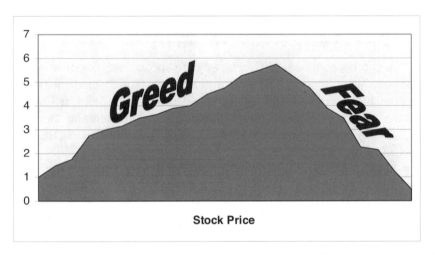

The investor held the stock because of greed. With every upward movement in the stock price, the investor congratulates himself and figures out how much money he has made. Perhaps the stock moved up fast and the investor thinks, "Gee, if it has moved up this much in only two months, imagine how high it will be after four months!"

•   **Rule 4**   •

Don't fall victim to the greed/fear trap.

This kind of greed in itself is not wrong. After all, why would anyone want to invest in a stock except for the greedy reason of making money? However, if greed keeps the investor from realizing a profit, it becomes a liability.

The final mistake the investor makes is letting this greed cause him to set a limit at $6. The investor wants to make a few more cents profit on each share. It doesn't matter that the stock has already made a fantastic profit, moving from $1 to $5.75 or +475 percent. If Murphy's Law (namely, anything that can go wrong will go wrong) is operating, the stock will never reach $6 before falling.

Greed has kept the investor from taking a profit because he is sure that the stock will continue to rise. Normally, when a stock moves up fast, it falls even faster. Once the stock starts to fall, the investor rationalizes, "I can't sell it at $5 because it was at $5.75 only yesterday; and I'm sure it will go back up." Then as the stock continues to fall, the investor becomes afraid to take the profit and reasons, "I can't sell the stock for only $3 when it was $5.75. It will go up again, and I'll miss out if I sell now."

This continues until the stock sometimes ends up below the original purchase price – perhaps at $0.50. Then the unhappy investor just wishes the stock would go back up to the original $1 purchase price so he can break even. (I'm sure that most investors can remember at least one time when they allowed themselves to become a victim of the greed/fear trap.)

PROTECTING YOURSELF FROM THE GREED/FEAR TRAP

Smart investors recognize how easy it is to fall into the greed/fear trap and learn to avoid it. They can protect themselves with a *stop limit* order, which instructs their broker to sell at a specified price or better but only after a given stop price has been reached or passed. The stop limit order avoids some of the risks of a *stop loss* order, which becomes a market order to sell at whatever the market price happens to be after the stop price has been reached.

As the stock price moves up, the smart investor raises the stop limit; but if the price experiences a serious drop, the stock should automatically be sold, to realize a profit. For example, if you bought a stock at $1 and it moved up to $2, you could call your broker and enter a stop limit order for $1.63. The stop limit should automatically sell your stock if it drops to $1.63. Not only would you have made a nice profit, you also protected yourself in case the stock price dropped further. As the stock price continues to move upward, your stop limit should be adjusted. Figure 4.2, on the next page, shows suggested stop limit prices.

Notice that the suggested stop limit for $2 is $1.63. It isn't set at $1.75 because that is where most investors would set it. To avoid a problem with selling your stock because too many other orders have also been entered, avoid setting stop losses on the even dollar, $0.50 or $0.25 amounts. At the $2, $3 and $4 prices the stop limit is $0.88 below the price; however, at the $6 through $10 level, it is $1.12 less. I set it at that point because the higher the stock price moves, the more volatility the stock has.

It's a balancing act. You want to protect your profit, yet you also don't want the stock sold just because the price jumped around a little. At higher prices, the major resistance point is usually at the dollar level. Therefore, if your stock hits $9, it may back off to $8 before continuing upward. If your stop limit had been set at $8.13, the stock would have been sold; and while you would have made a nice profit, there was potential for more. As you can see, it is a delicate job to set the stop loss high enough to keep your profit, but not so high that the stock gets sold when the price backs off somewhat.

Figure 4.2 Stop Limit Prices

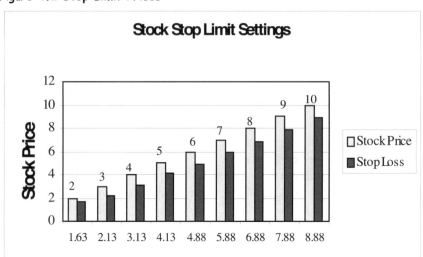

Understanding the investment process will help you learn the rules of how the investment game is played. Learning how and why companies raise capital, go public, and the factors that can affect a stock's price will help you make wiser investment decisions. It's also important to know when to take a profit and how to protect your profit.

There's a lot to learn and that's why I suggest specializing in one area of investments instead of trying to be a jack-of-all-trades. Specializing in quality stocks under $5 works for me. It can work for you too.

Chapter

5

Analyzing Stocks Easily
and Profitably

An investor's ultimate goal is to ascertain which investment affords the greatest profit potential. Some people let their brokers decide for them. Others pick a name that sounds familiar and has the ring of quality. Many follow the advice of chat lines on the Internet and a few have even tried the dartboard method of choosing stocks. (The investor throws a dart at a listing of stocks and buys the one that is hit.)

Choosing an investment is easy. However, if the investor wants to actually determine if the stock is a good investment, then he must analyze it. Making the effort to carefully check out an investment before buying it positions an individual in a select category of investors - the smart ones.

FUNDAMENTAL AND TECHNICAL ANALYSIS

While many variations exist, there are two major ways to analyze stocks. Fundamental analysis covers the study of all relevant financial information about a company that can influence the future course of its stock price. Technical analysis employs charts of the stock's price and trading volume and examines all factors related to the actual supply and demand for the company's stock.

Fundamental Analysis

This type of stock analysis evaluates the worthiness of a security by examining the company's tangible assets and financial strength. It focuses on elements such as book value, earnings per share and price-earnings (P/E) ratio, along with the stock's price in relation to its 52-week high/low range. Fundamental analysis considers past records of sales, earnings, cash, assets, products, management and markets when predicting future trends in the company's success or failure. Fundamental analysts may consider outside factors that could influence the company, such as the economic situation, government policy and the company's stature within its industry. The primary source of the data used in the analysis is the company's financial statements, which can be found in its annual, 10-K, 10-Q and quarterly reports.

Fundamental analysis had a great following during the 1930s depression when stocks were selling at perhaps 10 to 20 percent of their real value. *Security Analysis and Techniques* by Benjamin Graham and David Dodd, first printed in 1934, is the bible of fundamental analysis. In the book's preface the authors wrote of their decision to place "much emphasis upon distinguishing the investment from the speculative approach, upon setting up sound and workable tests of safety and upon an understanding of the rights and true interests of investors in senior securities and owners of common stock." Investors profited from following that premise in the 1930s, and I believe the same holds true today.

The goal of fundamental analysis is to examine a company's financial statement and other relevant information to discover if it is selling significantly below its worth. If so, the investor purchases the stock and waits until the rest of the world recognizes the stock's value. Sooner or later the stock price should move up closer to its true value. When the stock price goes up because everyone wants to buy it, that is the time to sell and use fundamental analysis to locate another undervalued company.

Former oilman and corporate raider, T. Boone Pickens used fundamental analysis to locate potential takeover candidates. Evaluating the fundamentals of a company allowed Pickens to determine if the breakup value was greater than the stock price. (The breakup value is what the stock could be worth if all the assets of the company were sold.) Pickens used this type of analysis very successfully to identify profitable takeover candidates.

Technical Analysis

Technical analysis usually thrives during times of economic prosperity or during bullish periods when stock prices are rising and trading profits are easy to make. In such times many analysts may revise their view of fundamental analysis and consider it out-of-date.

Figure 5.1 Price Chart

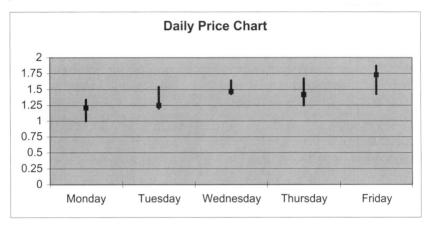

Technical analysts (or technicians) study all the factors related to the supply and demand of stocks. Through the use of stock charts, technicians seek various indicators that herald the change in the price or volume of a particular stock.

The major advantage of using technical analysis is that it creates a picture of the stock's price history. The simplest type of chart is a bar chart that indicates the high price, low price and closing price for the time period that can be calculated on a daily, weekly, monthly or yearly basis. Figure 5.1 is a bar chart that shows a week's worth of high, low and closing prices. A volume chart for a week may look like the one in Figure 5.2.

In technical analysis the investor is looking for patterns that could indicate which way the stock price will move. Figure 5.3 shows four basic patterns used in this type of analysis.

Technicians believe that since people make markets and people don't change that much, under similar conditions they will repeat their previous actions. Therefore, technical analysis involves the study of statistics for certain transactions to determine the direction of the future price of a stock or market. The technicians have concluded that those stocks or markets contain enough predictable elements to ensure the profitability of such studies over a period of time.

While a technician's charts are easy to read, using them correctly is more difficult. The analyst must anticipate where the stock is going, and the chart can be misleading, especially if it just shows a short period of time. Charting a stock for three to five years may show cyclical trends that occur around the same time each year. For example, a stock's price may rise shortly before it announces its quarterly financial results and then may fall rapidly thereafter. Determining such a pattern can give the investor an added profit-making edge.

Figure 5.2 Volume Chart

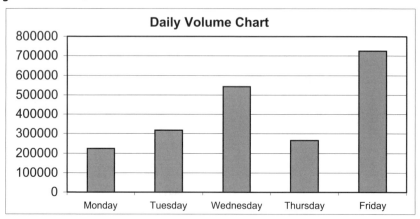

Technicians study the market using various indicators, including the evaluation of the economic variables within a market. Many stocks move with the market because they react to various supply-and-demand forces. That is, if investors want to buy more stock than is available, the price will go up. If more stock is being sold than there are buyers for the stock, the price will go down. Technical analysis can work well with stocks that tend to follow the market in general, such as the Dow Jones index stocks and other blue chips. However, I have found that this type of analysis doesn't work well with lower-priced stocks because they don't consistently follow the market.

Some technicians follow trading volume, for they believe that it can indicate whether or not a stock or a market is healthy. Presumably, the stock or market price will follow the volume trend. However, I have found that this assumption is not always true.

In the bull market of the late 90s, the hottest technical investment strategy was momentum buying. Technical analysts love buying stocks on upward movements, especially after they hit new 52-week highs. The idea is that since the stock price is moving up so fast, momentum will cause it to continue its upward movement.

In 1998 and 1999 momentum investors were a happy group because the market was so bullish that many stocks hit new highs and kept on going - just like they had hoped. However, the new millennium brought a reality check. Many investors, who continued to buy as those overvalued stocks pushed ever upward in the first quarter of 2000, found themselves vastly poorer by the end of the year. They learned first hand that buying high can lead to selling low. Momentum investors suffered tremendous losses over the first three years of the new millennium. Many investors ended up broke or left the market in disgust.

An interesting variation of technical analysis is the odd-lot theory, which is based on contrary opinion. The theory concludes that historically, odd lot traders (small investors who trade in less than 100-share quantities) are usually guilty of bad timing. When odd-lot volume rises in an up market, the odd lot analyst views it as a sign of technical weakness signaling a market reversal. Basically, the technician determines what the odd-lot traders are doing and does the opposite.

Figure 5.3 Four Basic Patterns Used in Technical Analysis

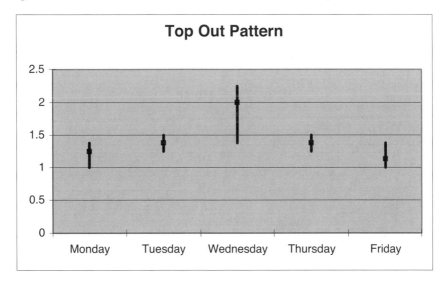

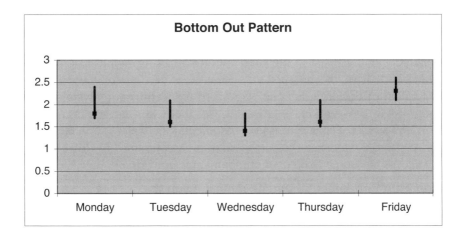

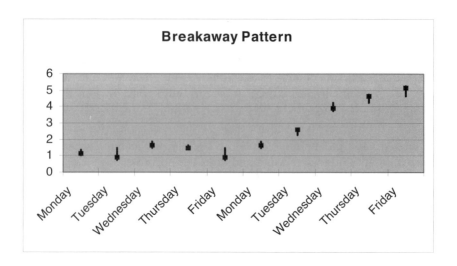

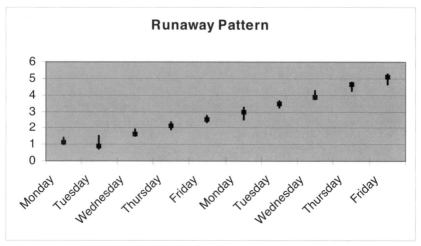

A very unusual theory for investment is called Random Walk. This investment philosophy discounts both fundamental and technical analysis. It concludes that at least in the short run, the market pricing is completely at random; there is no pattern because every price movement is independent of the previous one. So much for technical analysis! It also assumes that the market is efficient, so there are no underpriced or overpriced stocks. That dismisses fundamental analysis. So what is left? Well, you can always use the dartboard to pick your stocks. However, my best success has come from using fundamental analysis.

Comparing Fundamental and Technical Analysis

Let's look at fundamental and technical analysis in action. In April 1999 I recommended Aspect Telecommunications (NASDAQ - ASPT) at $6.44. Aspect provides software applications that integrate traditional telephone, e-mail, voicemail, Web, fax, wireless business communications and voice-over-IP. Businesses use its products to improve customer satisfaction, reduce operating costs, gather market intelligence and increase revenue.

In August of 1998 Aspect had been a high flyer as momentum technical buyers frantically purchased shares at $38. A good portion of those momentum buyers got scared and sold when the price plunged. Eventually Aspect hit $6.44 where I thought it was a good buy point.

I liked the stock because the Company had great fundamentals, with revenues of $512 million and a net income of $32 million ($0.61 per share). Aspect also had almost $200 million or $4 per share in cash. The purchase of 372,000 shares at $7 per share ($2.6 million) by one of Aspect's directors was an indication of Management's confidence in the Company. The Company had good sales and earnings and a strong balance sheet. The icing on the cake was the stock was selling near its 52-week low price.

While I thought Aspect was a great bargain at $6.44, a technician wouldn't have been impressed because of its price's downward movement. In fact, I spoke with an analyst shortly before I recommended Aspect, and he advised to stay away. Luckily I didn't take his advice because the telecommunications industry soared in February and March 2000, and Aspect skyrocketed to $70 for almost a 1,000 percent gain.

Ironically, when the stock took off, it gained the interest of technicians who began jumping on the bandwagon, when many of my newsletter subscribers were jumping off and taking tremendous profits.

Aspect Telecommunications is a prime example of the benefits of using fundamental analysis to discover a quality investment. Instead of waiting until a stock's price and volume increase dramatically on technical charts to indicate that it is a good buy, fundamental analysis allows the investor to buy the stock at a much lower price. That is the main reason I use fundamental analysis and perhaps why *The CHEAP Investor* has recommended so many stocks well before the Wall Street analysts become interested in them.

DELVING INTO ANNUAL, 10-K, 10-Q AND QUARTERLY REPORTS AND PRESS RELEASES

To analyze a stock, you need several publications that you can obtain on the Internet or directly from the company by either calling or writing. You need the company's annual report, the 10-K and 10-Q reports, its latest quarterly report and any press releases. The information in these reports can help you determine whether or not a stock is a potentially profitable investment.

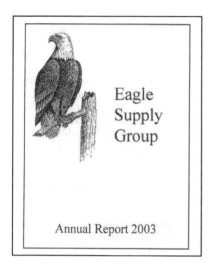

Eagle
Supply
Group

Annual Report 2003

Annual Reports

The annual report is a brochure that reports the company's financial condition. The SEC requires that the annual report be distributed to shareholders each year. In addition to financial reports and notes from an independent certified public accountant, the report commonly contains a summary of the products or services, a progress report, comments from the president and chairperson on the company's financial and industry status and reports on corporate expansion and new products.

Most annual reports are designed by the company's advertising or public relations department to promote the company to the reader. Generally written in easy-to-understand language, the annual report explains the company's products and goals. It can be very basic and printed in black and white, or it can be flashy and include colors photos on high quality paper to impress shareholders. A company with poor financial results may invest in an extremely expensive-looking annual report, hoping that it will give the impression that it is a good investment. Don't be fooled.

Financial Statement

While annual reports vary greatly, they all contain a financial statement that is an audited, written record of the company's financial status. The financial statement consists of five parts:

- consolidated balance sheet
- income statement
- statement of changes in financial position
- statement of retained earnings
- notes to the financial statements

Consolidated Balance Sheet A company's balance sheet presents its financial position in detail. It shows the balance of its various types of assets, liabilities and shareholder equity as of a specific date. The assets are basically what the company owns, the liabilities are what it owes and the shareholders' equity is the value after all the liabilities are subtracted from the assets. Shareholders' equity per share is determined by dividing the shareholders' equity by the number of shares outstanding.

Income Statement This report provides information concerning the total revenues, costs, expenses and net earnings from operations.

Statement of Changes in Financial Position The statement presents information concerning the company's operating, financing and investing activities. The statement indicates any changes in the company's financial position during the year.

Statement of Retained Earnings This is a combined statement of the company's yearly income and retained earnings. Retained earnings are the total amount of cumulative net profits reinvested in the corporation after the payment of dividends.

Notes to the Financial Statement This final report provides an explanation of specific items in the financial statement. The notes are extremely important, for they may contain positive or negative information that could have a significant impact on the company. In many cases companies will use this section to hide negative information that must be disclosed. As a potential investor, you will want to read this section carefully.

What to Look For in the Annual Report

There is no standardized form for annual reports, so I can only generalize. On the inside of the annual report's front cover there usually is a corporate profile detailing the company's main areas of business. If the company's earnings are very positive, the report will probably contain a section on selected financial data comparing three to five years of sales (or revenues), net income, net income per share and the number of shares outstanding. Have the sales and net income improved compared to the previous year or years?

Financial Highlights Section Many annual reports contain a financial highlights section that details sales, earnings, assets, liabilities and shareholders' equity. Look for increases in the assets and in the shareholders' equity and decreases in the liabilities. Read the notes below the financial data to see if there is anything extremely positive or negative.

Letter to the Shareholders The letter to the shareholders is written by the president or chairperson of the board. It details what has happened to the company during the past year and presents the goals that the company hopes to accomplish during the next year. Typically, the letter is extremely positive, looking on the bright side regardless of the company's performance during the past year.

Notes to the Financial Statement If you like what you have seen so far, find the section in the financial statement called the "Notes to the Financial Statement" and read it carefully. A section on litigation is usually near the end of the annual report. It is not unusual for lawsuits to be brought against a company; however, you should investigate to see whether the company has insurance to cover the cost if it loses any lawsuit. If the company is suing another company or individual for a large amount of money, this could prove extremely positive if the company wins. (For example, MCI received a big boost by suing AT&T and winning.)

Accountant's Letter Look at the accountant's letter. Reading this letter will often give you some insight into the company's health. The paragraph starting with "In our opinion" is especially important. Is the company's accountant a well-known accounting firm? If so, that is usually a positive factor.

Number of Shareholders The number of shareholders can also be important, and a stock with at least 1,000 shareholders is best. A large number of shareholders indicate that there are many small shareholders. When selling occurs in a stock with only a small number of shareholders, it can cause the stock to be more volatile, especially on the downside.

Market Information The market-information section indicates which exchange the stock is traded on and its symbol and gives two years (by quarters) of its high and low prices. The example below shows that the high and the low price may vary quite a bit depending on the quarter.

High and Low Bid Prices
(Year-end December 31, 2003)

	High	Low
Fourth quarter	$6.50	$3.13
Third quarter	3.50	2.75
Second quarter	5.38	2.25
First quarter	3.88	3.75

High and Low Bid Prices
(Year-end December 31, 2002)

	High	Low
Fourth quarter	$5.00	$2.75
Third quarter	4.25	3.50
Second quarter	5.00	2.13
First quarter	3.00	2.38

It is not uncommon for a stock to trade at higher prices during certain quarters. In the previous example the stock traded for a higher price in the second and fourth quarters. If you check the company's sales and earnings for these quarters, you may find a correlation between the sales and earnings and the stock price. Many companies experience seasonal sales, and those quarters may be historically better than others. For example, a company involved in retail sales will probably post its largest sales in the October through December quarter due to holiday shopping.

Form 10-K

This report is filed with the SEC by all companies listed on the NYSE, Amex, NASDAQ and OTC Bulletin Board. The SEC requires that certain information be listed in the 10-K and that it be filed within 90 days after the close of the fiscal year. Because the 10-K is written by the financial department and sent to the SEC, it gives more explicit information about the company and its divisions, finances and products than does the annual report.

The 10-K may seem complicated at first, but it becomes easier to read with practice. It normally includes the following information about the company:

- Industry
- Competitors
- Regulations
- Patents and trademarks
- Accessibility of raw materials
- Location of each division, office, franchise, etc.
- Order backlog
- Research and development
- Environmental regulations
- Employees
- Foreign and domestic operations
- Export sales
- Description of properties, including location, size, cost and lease expiration date
- Marketing
- Employment agreements
- Full information on all legal proceedings
- Company stock market information
- Complete annual financial statements
- Liquidity and capital resources

- Management's description and analysis of the financial condition and results of operations

- Expenses e.g., why they changed and specific factors that caused the change

- Information and background on the directors and executive officers

- Executive compensation, including profit-sharing, bonus and retirement plans

- Employee stock ownership, including the number of shares owned and the price paid by all officers and directors

- Information on various types of securities offered by the company

What is important to the investor? While all this information is interesting, some is more important to the stock price than others. If you don't have the annual report, then check the 10-K's financial statements and look for increasing revenues and earnings. Read to determine if there are any lawsuits that could either be very positive or negative for the company. Look at the stock market information to see if the price has any cyclical tendencies.

Check the management's compensation. Is it out of line with the company's finances? (Many companies have been bled dry by outlandish management salaries and stock-option or bonus programs.) The 10-K will contain the pertinent information if a Form 8-K has recently been filed with the SEC. A Form 8-K is required by the SEC following any event that affects the company's financial situation.

Learn if any warrants are outstanding. If so, what are the exercise price and the expiration date? Does the company plan a public or private offering of stock? In either case this could affect the price of the stock, for there will be more shares outstanding to dilute the value of the stock once the offering is completed or the warrant is exercised.

Always check the company's cash situation. If the cash assets are extremely low or the company is in a deficit position, it may have to raise capital in the near future with a public or private offering that could severely weaken the current shares' value.

If you are seriously considering purchasing a stock, make sure you read the Management's Description segment of the 10-K. That section gives an overall view of the company's condition.

Form 10-Q

This report is filed with the SEC 45 days after the end of the quarter. It is similar to the 10-K but much smaller. It, of course, presents the latest quarterly financial results. Check these numbers for changes (both positive and negative) that should be considered when analyzing the company's investment potential.

The 10-Q contains management's analysis of the quarter, any 8-K filings and the notes to the financial statements. All of these should be examined. Basically, you are looking for any changes in the company's overall picture.

Quarterly Report

The quarterly report is sent to the shareholders to describe the current financial condition of the company. It contains the sales, net income, net income per share, number of shares outstanding and sometimes the shareholder's equity and compares it with the previous year's quarter. Analyze the figures for improvements. A short letter to the shareholders may be included. It may comment on the quarterly figures and describe any new developments during the past three months.

Press Releases

Readily found on the Internet, press releases can help you learn more about the company including its products, business agreements and contracts. Usually the company will issue its quarterly sales and earnings report in a press release along with comments from its management. I prefer to see the company issue three or four press releases each month to help get its story out to Wall Street.

GETTING THE FACTS BEFORE YOU INVEST

Many people lose money in the stock market because they invest based on the word of a relative, friend or broker. Often the information is completely wrong because each time it was passed from one person to the next, something was added or deleted. If it was passed through enough people, the original information has probably been totally distorted. Even brokers experience problems, for many times they don't analyze a stock themselves but rely on their brokerage firm's analysts. This is fine except that the analysts may not have the time to update their information as often as they should, so the information the broker gets may be obsolete.

If you have the annual report, 10-K, 10-Q, quarterly report and press releases, you probably have as much, or more, information than most stockbrokers and analysts have. Using that information wisely can make the difference between making and losing money. By doing your research first, you will know that the information is accurate. This step can greatly increase your odds of making a profit.

FINDING THE NEXT SUPER STOCK

Taking the time to obtain the various company reports, reading them carefully and analyzing the stock's strong and weak points to see if it is a good buy is well worth the effort.

My ultimate goal when researching a company's stock is to find one with perfect criteria. The company must provide superior products or services. Its management team should possess the expertise to efficiently market that product or service. It strives to improve sales and earnings, continue expansion with new products or services and search for new markets to penetrate. If the company's stock is at a good low price, it fulfills the qualifications for the next potential super stock.

The following are the three key items that can almost guarantee a stock-price jump:

- The company is producing record sales.
- The company is achieving record earnings.
- The company's stock price is near its 52-week low.

Several of my big stock winners fit these criteria when I researched them. Here are a few:

Company Name	Recommended Price	High Since Recommendation
Envirodyne Industries	$2.81	$80.00 (buyout)
Avigen, Inc.	2.25	89.00
Idec Pharmaceutical	5.00	*225.00
PrePaid Legal	1.31	48.75
Hauppauge Digital	2.81	*96.00
*Equivalent price after stock splits		

My statistics indicate that, if you find a stock that satisfies the previously mentioned three criteria, your chances of that stock moving upward are more than 90 percent. If the company continues to achieve record sales and earnings, the chances are excellent that the stock price will soar.

The great advantage of this approach is that you buy the stock long before the Wall Street analysts are interested. In fact, by the time many become interested in the stock (because it has moved up so high), it will be time for you to think about taking your profit. If you follow my lead and carefully analyze the fundamentals of any stock you are considering for an investment, perhaps you can find the next super stock and reap a tremendous profit as well.

Chapter

Mastering CHEAP Stocks

For more than 25 years I have written about investing in quality, low priced stocks or as I call them, CHEAP stocks. One key truth I learned is that the small investor, with a limited amount of capital, obviously needs a higher percent of return than an investor with a large amount of investment capital. For example, if a small investor with only $3,000 and a larger investor with $200,000 invest in a security with a guaranteed annual return of 10 percent, the small investor receives only $300 per year while the large investor collects $20,000.

Large investor: $200,000 x 10% = $20,000
Small investor: $3,000 x 10% = $300

Because the smaller investor is starting with a more modest amount of capital, he needs a higher rate of return (30, 40 or 50 percent) to help that capital grow. I spent years researching differently priced stocks to find which ones may be more advantageous for the small investor. Through the practical application of various investment theories, I concluded that CHEAP stocks (under $5 per share) offer a far greater growth potential, which the small investor needs. The higher-priced, blue chip stocks have, for the most part, already experienced their major growth cycle and thus do not provide a high enough rate of return. In fact, many of those stocks tend to be overpriced, and their prices probably will decrease.

```
┌─────────────────────────────────────────────────┐
│  •          Rule 5          •                     │
│          Avoid high-priced stocks.                │
└─────────────────────────────────────────────────┘
```

Many higher-priced stocks are so expensive that it is virtually impossible for the stocks to double in price. CHEAP stocks offer greater growth potential than the long-established, high-priced stocks. My research proves that it is easier for a CHEAP stock to soar from $1 to $10 than it is for a $50 stock to move to $500.

TREMENDOUS POTENTIAL VERSUS BLUE CHIPS

Again and again I have seen quality, low-priced stocks far outpace the blue chips. I think that it is much easier for a company such as Value City Department Stores (NYSE – VCD) to move from $1.75 to $3.50 than for IBM (NYSE – IBM) to double from $90 to $180. I have discovered that people who made fortunes owning today's blue chip stocks bought them years ago when the stocks were much cheaper, and the investors could buy many more shares.

The small investor who has only $3,000 to invest must have his money work hard. While it may be tempting to buy blue chip stocks because they are "safer," they are so expensive that $3,000 will not buy many shares. Also, what may be a safe blue chip today, can easily be a loser tomorrow. All stocks carry some risk.

```
┌─────────────────────────────────────────────────┐
│  •          Rule 6          •                     │
│  Controlling larger amounts of shares will translate │
│             into higher profits.                  │
└─────────────────────────────────────────────────┘
```

For example, you have $3,000 to invest. You can either buy Value City at $1.75 or IBM at $90. As you can see, you would be able to purchase 1,714 shares of Value City and not quite 34 shares of IBM.

$3,000 ÷ $1.75 per share for Value City   = 1,714 shares
$3,000 ÷ $90 per share for IBM   = 34 shares

If both stocks increase by $1, your profit would be much greater with Value City than with IBM because you can own more shares. As you can see, the more shares you own, the higher your profit.

1,714 shares of Value City x $1   = $1,714
34 shares of IBM x $1   = $34

Although the Wall Street media report stock movements in dollars and cents, I believe it is important to figure your profits in percentages. Think about it; when it comes to financial matters, almost everyone uses percentages. The IRS taxes your income by a variable percent, your bank lends money to buy a new home or car and charges a certain percent interest and even your credit card company expects you to pay a percentage finance charge. Doesn't it make sense to look at your investment profits in percentages too?

It's easy to be impressed by a stock that has jumped a few dollars in one day. Because blue chip stocks cost so much, the actual profit may not be as great as it seems. Wall Street gets excited when IBM moves up $5 to $95, and the jump will be reported on almost all the business news programs. However, a $1.75 stock that moves up $0.50 is usually forgotten. In fact, IBM moved up less than 6 percent, while Value City rose almost 29 percent! Which would you rather have owned?

•   Rule 7   •

**Always look at profits and losses in percentages,
not in dollars and cents.**

In the previous example, if Value City increased by only $1.50 and IBM jumped $15, it might look like IBM performed better. If you figure the profit percentages, however, you will see a different story. Value City's $1.50 increase is an 86 percent profit, and IBM's huge $15 increase is a mere 17 percent profit.

1,714 Value City shares x $1.50 increase   = $2,571 profit
$2,571 profit ÷ $3,000 purchase price   = 86%

34 IBM shares x $15 increase   = $510 profit
$510 profit ÷ $3,000 purchase price   = 17%

Because you are comparing the same amount of investment ($3,000), it is pretty easy to see which stock gave you the greater profit. However, it would be rare that you would invest the same amount of money in all your stocks. Therefore, looking at the percent of profit is the only accurate way to compare just how well your investments have done. These examples illustrate three important points:

- *Many people lose money in the stock market because they invest in the wrong price stocks.* Typically, you can make more money with a quality $1.75 stock than with a blue chip, $90 stock. That's because the profit potential is far greater with the growing $1.75 stock than with the mature $90 stock.

- *An important key to making money in the stock market is the number of shares you control.* A $3,000 investment can control 1,714 shares of a $1.75 stock and less than 34 shares of a $90 stock.

- *Always look at profits and losses in percentages, not dollars and cents.* If you had just looked at how many dollars Value City and IBM had risen, you would have been tempted to say that IBM had done quite a bit better. In reality, Value City was a significantly more profitable investment.

DIVERSIFICATION IN GRADES OF SPECULATION

Every investor knows that diversifying into different stocks is important. Usually the investor will buy stocks in various industries and consider himself diversified. This is a good start, but I like to add another dimension when investing in CHEAP stocks. I found that stocks under $5 tend to separate into three levels of speculation.

For the most part, stocks under $1.50 are the riskiest and most volatile investments. These include companies listed on the NASDAQ SmallCaps and the OTC Bulletin Board. Because they are so volatile, they can easily shoot up 200, 300, 400 percent or more.

The problem is the stocks move up quickly and fall back even faster. Investors must take some profit off the table or those profits may vanish. Winners Internet, Fonix and Dauphin are great examples. Winners Internet soared from my recommendation at $0.56 to $8 or +1,329 percent. Today, the stock is trading on the pink sheets for less than a penny. Fonix shot from its $0.25 recommendation price to $3.38 or +1,252 percent. Fonix currently trades at $0.14 after a one for forty reverse stock split. Dauphin Technologies exploded from $0.27 to $12.50 or +4,529 percent. Dauphin is now trading at $0.25. Because of their volatility, these stocks are very speculative. Many savvy investors trade CHEAP stocks like these for profits of 50 to 100 percent or more.

The second group generally trades from $1.50 to $3.00. The stocks tend to be higher caliber but are less volatile. They can take longer to move and impatient investors may get tired of waiting for a move and sell. One subscriber I talked to had 5,000 shares of Avigen Inc. (NASDAQ – AVGN) at $2.25 (recommended January 1998) and sold at that price because the stock didn't move. He should have held on because Avigen hit $89 in March 2000.

The third group of CHEAP stocks sells between $3 and $6. Usually the highest quality companies, they may be turnaround candidates. While they are even less volatile, they can be big winners if they eventually reach $10 or more and momentum buyers get excited about them. Two recent examples of this are Aspect Technology (NASDAQ – ASPT), which soared from $6.44 to $70.00 and Summit Technology (NASDAQ – BEAM), which skyrocketed from $3.94 to $29.38. Success stories like these are the reason why I suggest varying your investment speculations.

LOCATING A CHEAP INVESTMENT

Finding the companies to research as potential investments involves actively searching for them. Look at companies where you live or work. It is extremely easy to get information and see how well a company's product is doing when it is located nearby. You can just call or stop by its business office to request information. One of my Chicago area subscribers called and asked me to meet with the management of a local firm, Dauphin Technology (OTCBB - DNTK). Dauphin was developing a hand-held computer that used voice recognition and other unique features. It was a very speculative stock selling for about $0.27. I met with the management, liked the potential and recommended it, at that low price. Over the next year Dauphin soared more than 45 times to $12.50.

Always be on the lookout for new investment opportunities. If a company's product or service impresses you, chances are others will be impressed as well. Several years ago a new restaurant, Benihana, opened in our area. I took my wife and some friends to check it out. It was a Japanese restaurant with Teppanyaki cooking. Each table had its own chef who rapidly sliced the meat and vegetables and grilled them in the middle of the table. The delicious food and entertainment by the fast talking/chopping chef was a unique treat. That dining experience piqued my curiosity about the company. Talking with the restaurant manager, I discovered Benihana, Inc. traded on the NASDAQ (symbol BNHNA). Upon further investigation, I was surprised to learn the stock was trading for a measly $0.75. I recommended it in the newsletter at that price. A couple years later Benihana hit a new high of $17 or +2,167 percent! That's quite a return for following through on an investment hunch.

A good source for potential investments is the business section in your local newspaper. You should also glance through *The Wall Street Journal, Investor's Business Daily* and *Barron's.* (All three newspapers should be available in your local library.)

Another way to find potential investments is to subscribe to a stock newsletter. Newsletters can be a great source of investments; however, you will want to do some research before you buy. Read the small print to see if the newsletter is being paid with stock or as a "consultant" to write the recommendation. In that case, the recommendation is not objective. It's a paid advertisement.

Avoid newsletters that offer only one buy recommendation. If the newsletter has a good following, recommending only one stock will almost guarantee that the stock will soar in price. However, the stock may move up so quickly that the average investor will probably pay a much higher price. When a stock moves up quickly, chances are it will fall back even faster. Make sure that the newsletter lists a specific buy price and gives the Website and/or name, address and telephone number of the company so you can contact it for further information.

Listing Stocks for Further Research

A good place to find and research bargain stocks is the Internet or your library. You can also use *Investor's Business Daily* or *Barron's* to search through the NYSE, Amex and NASDAQ stocks, and make a list of all profitable companies under $5 near their 52-week low price. I use the format shown in Figure 6.1 to gather all the pertinent information. (When you hear of an interesting company, add it to this checklist.) Once you have a list of potential investments, research them on the Internet. One of the best Internet resources is Yahoo Finance at http://finance.yahoo.com/. From that Website, you can request a basic stock quote on your potential investment. The stock quote screen offers a wide variety of information including financials, company profile, news, charts and SEC filings.

Figure 6.1 Potential Investments

52 Week High	Low	Company Name	Stock Symbol	Current Price	No Good	Potential Investment

You can also check other informational sources in the library such as *Standard & Poor's Stock Guide, Value Line,* and *Standard & Poor's Stock Reports.* These references will give you a synopsis of what a particular company does, its sales and earnings and its stock price over the past few years. Using that information, you can either cross the company off your potential investments list or add it to your investment-grade stocks list. (See Figure 6.2.)

Figure 6.2 Investment-Grade Stocks

52 Week High	Low	Company Name	Stock Symbol	Current Price	Positive Aspects	Negative Aspects

The stocks on the investment-grade list need further research. Use all the techniques described in the previous chapter to analyze these stocks.

Once you have carefully analyzed the investment candidates and eliminated those that don't qualify, you should have a group of quality, low-priced stocks as potential investments.

NASDAQ Stocks

Buying and selling stocks that are listed on the NASDAQ market is different from buying and selling stocks listed on the New York and American exchanges. While stocks listed on the NYSE and Amex are quoted with just one price, NASDAQ stocks have a *bid* and *asked* price. If a stock is listed as $1 bid and $1.05 asked, this means that if you wanted to buy the stock, you would pay the $1.05 asked price. If you wished to sell the stock, you would receive the $1 bid price. The $0.05 difference between the bid and asked prices is called the *spread.*

The spread on a NASDAQ stock can indicate how actively the stock is traded. If a stock has a small spread, say $0.01, then it trades a lot. However, if a stock doesn't trade very much, in many cases, the spread will be large. It is not uncommon to see a thinly traded stock with a $0.50 bid price and a $1 asked price. As an investor, don't even consider a stock with such a large spread, because you would have to pay $1 to buy and would get only $0.50 if you sold. The stock would have to move up $0.50 or 100 percent before you break even!

Whenever you are considering a NASDAQ stock, always check the spread. Avoid all NASDAQ stocks with spreads greater than those listed in the chart below.

Target NASDAQ Stock Spreads	
Stocks between $.01 and $.25	$ .005 to .01 spread
Stocks between $.26 and $.75	$ .01 to $.02 spread
Stocks between $.76 and $ 2.00	$.02 to $.05 spread
Stocks $2 and up	$.03 to $.10 spread

OTC Bulletin Board Stocks

Several years ago, the NASD created the electronic Bulletin Board for stocks trading under $1. NASD made it extremely difficult for brokers to trade or recommend Bulletin Board stocks. I believe the NASD did this to deter investors from penny stocks (stocks selling for less than $1 per share), in the hope that instead they would buy higher priced stocks. This strategy seemed to work for a while, and then the Internet changed everything.

With the ease of gathering information and the low cost of connecting to the Internet, investors flocked to this new way to track their investments. On the Internet, they discovered numerous Websites and chat rooms devoted to investing. It opened their eyes to new realms of investments.

Penny stocks were very attractive since investors could buy a lot of shares for a small investment. If their old broker didn't want to take an order for penny stocks, there were plenty of brokers on the Internet who would. In 1999 and 2000, the on-line brokerage industry exploded, and many investors felt pretty sophisticated as they traded their OTC BB stocks on their home computer.

Instead of withering away, the OTC BB created a huge market for penny stocks. Just be aware that all stocks selling for under $1 are very speculative. There are some great companies listed on the Bulletin Board, but there have also been several scams. It's important to do your homework and check each company before investing. Look for companies that trade large daily volumes of at least 100,000 to 500,000 shares. Be careful of the bid and asked spread. They should follow the chart below.

Target OTC BB Stock Spreads	
Stocks between $.01 and $.20	$0.001 to .005 spread
Stocks between $.21 and $.50	$.005 to $.01 spread
Stocks between $.51 and $.75	$.01 to $.02 spread
Stocks $.76 and up	$.03 spread

Drawbacks to OTC BB Stocks

While OTC BB stocks are better than pink sheets, they are still in one of the lowest ranks of stocks. In general, if a stock doesn't have the assets to get listed on any of the more prestigious exchanges, it falls into the OTC BB category. An OTC BB stock may have a great story about its potential; however, I personally can't think of one that has become a major corporation.

It can be difficult to get any written information (including financial data) about an OTC BB stock. A company listed on the OTC BB only files financials once a year. Make sure that the stock is a reporting company and that it has filed its latest yearly financials with the SEC before investing.

OTC Pink-Sheet Stocks

Pink-sheet stocks originally got their name from the color of the pages of the National Quotation Bureau's publication that listed its bid and asked prices. Thousands of stocks do not meet the more stringent requirements to get listed on NASDAQ or the OTC Bulletin Board and are therefore listed on the pink sheets. The big negative factor is pink sheet stocks are very thinly traded. In addition, there are no real bid and asked prices for pink sheet stocks. I recommend staying away from pink sheet stocks.

Penny Stocks

A penny stock by definition is one that sells under $1. Before the recent bear market, penny stocks were considered the lowest of the low. Things changed in the first three years of the new millennium as several well-known stocks that were former Wall Street favorites found themselves in the embarrassing position of qualifying as penny stocks. On the NYSE alone, companies like Nortel, Silicon Graphics, Foster Wheeler, W. R. Grace and Atlas Air Worldwide plummeted below $1. The NASDAQ exchange resorted to revising its listing requirements rather than delist the hundreds of companies that had fallen below its $1 price minimum. Amazingly some of those companies were selling at prices ranging from $50 to $100 in early 2000!

The penny stocks that I'm concerned with in this section are the ones that have little revenues, huge losses and are listed on the OTC Bulletin Board or pink sheets. Their low price makes penny stocks extremely attractive to individual investors. However, investors should be aware that the vast majority of stock scams have been stocks in this category.

When a broker tells you about a great little company selling for only $0.75 per share, many investors think, "Gee, the stock is so inexpensive. What can I lose?" Unfortunately, you can lose your whole investment.

Many penny stocks may seem low priced but are actually tremendously overpriced! Because penny stocks are not widely traded, there may be a large spread between the price you pay to buy the stock and the price at which you can sell it. That $0.75 stock may have a $0.25 spread, which is exorbitant. In addition, it is very difficult to discover if the stock is near its high or low. If that $0.75 stock has a 52-week low of $0.10 and a high of $0.88, it's not such a great deal.

Often a penny stock company will have an outrageous market capitalization of $50 million (number of shares multiplied by stock price), yet it does not have $4 million in assets to become listed on the NASDAQ. To me, that indicates that the stock is vastly overpriced.

Investors who want to reduce risk buy stocks that are at least listed on the NASDAQ system. If a company is listed on the NYSE, Amex or NASDAQ exchanges, you know it has met stringent requirements that make it a less risky investment.

THE PITFALLS OF HOT TIPS

Traditionally, hot stock tips used to come from brokers cold calling prospective investors. This was chillingly depicted in the movie *Boiler Room*. If you haven't seen it, rent it! It's an eye-opening movie all investors should watch.

Today's hot stock tip can come from many sources including friends, family, taxi drivers, chat rooms, and barbers. I believe the biggest mistake an investor can make is not fully researching a stock before buying shares. Most investors ask the obvious questions of what does the company do and how healthy is its financial state. However, if the investor had asked these three questions, in many cases he would not have bought the stock and therefore not have lost money.

1. *What is the company's stock symbol?* You'll need the symbol to pull up the current stock price and company information on the Internet.

2. *Where is the stock traded?* If the stock is traded on the NYSE, Amex, NASDAQ or OTC Bulletin Board, that's fine. If it trades on the OTC pink-sheets or a foreign exchange (including the Vancouver, Ontario, Canadian, London, Berlin or Australian exchanges), say, "Thanks, but no thanks."

3. *Where is the stock's current price in relation to its 52-week high and low price?* Most investors fail to find out the answer to this question and wind up purchasing a stock at its high price. This mistake can mean huge losses when the price falls.

Hot tips are worth exactly what you paid for them. It's possible that the person does know what he's talking about, but don't assume. Check the stock before investing!

THREE CRITERIA FOR SUCCESSFUL STOCK PICKS

When I decided to specialize in quality, low-priced stocks, I wanted to discover the best way to analyze those stocks to weed out the poor investments. After years of studying fundamental analysis of blue chip stocks, I modified those methods of analysis for low-priced stocks. This successful technique for picking bargain stocks contains the following three criteria that a stock should meet to have the most profit potential:

- Increasing sales
- Increasing earnings (profits)
- Selling near its 52-week low price

In July 1997, I recommended Hauppauge Digital (NASDAQ – HAUP) at $2.88. The company manufactures and markets digital video products for the PC market. At that time, Hauppauge had posted a 58 percent increase in six-month sales and an enormous 123 percent rise in net income when compared to the previous year. In addition, the stock was selling at its 52-week low price. Over the next three years, Hauppauge soared to $96 (equivalent price after 2/1 stock split) or +3,200 percent! Ironically, at $2.88 Wall Street didn't like Hauppauge Digital, but at $96, it was on most major brokerage firms' buy lists.

Increasing sales and earnings show that demand exists for a company's products and that it can cover the additional costs to expand facilities to continue its growth. More importantly, increasing earnings (profits) indicate that the company is successfully marketing its product. Year after year of increasing profits signify that the company has the potential to move from a blue CHEAP stock to a blue chip stock.

The low stock price is the most important factor. Because most stocks are cyclical, moving from near their 52-week low to near their 52-week high, it just doesn't make sense to buy them when they are at the high point. I heartily disagree with brokers who call their clients and tell them about a great stock that is setting new price records and recommend that they buy it at the new record price because "it should continue to go higher."

It is not uncommon to analyze a stock and determine that it is a good investment, yet decide the stock price is too high. If that's the case, occasionally check the stock price. When it moves down, re-examine the company to make sure that no negative news is causing the price to drop. If there isn't any negative news, you have a great investment opportunity – a quality company at a low price.

The previously mentioned three factors are very important to the success of your investment. Having the patience and discipline to wait to purchase that quality stock near its 52-week low should guarantee a potential profit about 80 percent of the time.

LITTLE COMPETITION MEANS VERY HIGH PROFITS

In just about any business environment, a company that offers a good product with little competition will be extremely prosperous. Perhaps one reason I have been so successful recommending quality stocks under $5 is that there is very little Wall Street competition.

Most analysts and brokers with major brokerage firms ignore stocks under $5. The majority of their recommendations are for stocks $20 and higher. At the other end of the spectrum, very few analysts even look at the highly speculative penny and pink-sheet stocks. Investing in quality stocks under $5 is often forgotten and left to the few of us who are smart enough to recognize the potential.

When a good quality stock is at $1 a share, Wall Street usually doesn't get excited about it until it has moved up above $5. One such company was Atari Corporation (NASDAQ – ATAR), which I recommended at $1. This well-known company is a major player in the computer entertainment field. It was selling for one-half of its book value; yet it had good cash assets, a new product line that would shortly be introduced and great profit potential. Hardly anyone was interested in the stock. It had to move up to $11 before the major brokerage firms began to recommend it.

Atari eventually hit a high of $12.75. Investors who waited for their brokers to call them with the recommendation at $11 probably got burned, as the stock fell to $6 shortly thereafter. However, if those investors had bought at my $1 recommendation, they could have made a 1,175 percent profit! Atari illustrates how the investor can be the big winner by purchasing a quality, low-priced stock before Wall Street becomes interested in it. Atari had already moved up 1,000 percent from my $1 recommendation by the time the major Wall Street firms recommended it at $11. It pays to keep your eyes open for good investments.

HOW TO FOLLOW YOUR STOCKS

In Chapter 1, you learned how to read a stock page. Following your stock involves checking the price twice a week or more, if the stock is volatile. There are several ways you can get a price quote. If you have Internet access, you can easily follow most stocks on any of the various stock quote services. If the stock is listed in *The Wall Street Journal, Investor's Business Daily* or your local newspaper, you can study it every day. You can also call your broker for a price quote, but he won't appreciate it if you frequently call when the market is open and prevent your broker from making a commission. Unless you are considering selling the stock, I suggest calling for a quote after the market has closed. However you do it, it is important that you follow the prices of your stocks so you don't miss any opportunities to make a profit.

Chapter

$$7$$

Mastering Turnaround Stocks

One goal that all stock investors share is to find a stock with the potential to be the next Microsoft or Wal-Mart. This is a fine goal, though most investors will never achieve it. However, there is one investment area that can provide great profit and self-satisfaction – turnaround stocks. Turnaround stocks tend to be the most profitable of all the CHEAP stocks because many originally were high-priced glamour stocks. When they start to bounce back, investors remember them from before and quickly jump on the stock bandwagon. Turnarounds can be the most rewarding investments.

By definition a turnaround stock is a quality company whose price has plunged, usually in response to negative news. The investor's first task is to determine if the news will permanently affect the company or just temporarily weaken it.

In many cases the negative news will cause no permanent harm and the stock will rebound in a matter of weeks or months. When an investor correctly determines the low point where the panic selling stops and the bargain buying begins, it can be a very enjoyable and profitable occasion.

CarMax (KMX), listed on the NYSE, is a great example of how investors can profit from turnarounds. It was a hot IPO (initial public offering) in 1998 at $20 and many institutional buyers jumped on the CarMax bandwagon. The stock moved up to $22. Then AutoNation (the largest auto superstore in the industry) had to scale back and CarMax suffered losses.

These negative events caused institutional selling and CarMax's price slid to a low of $1.50 over the next couple of years. I recommended CarMax in the February 2000 issue of *The CHEAP Investor* because I liked the Company's fundamentals. CarMax pioneered the auto superstore concept in 1993, offering low, no-haggle prices and a broad range of new and used cars. It had a book value of $15.10 per share and had become profitable. For nine months, it posted sales of $1.5 billion and a net income of $0.03 per share.

I thought CarMax was a great bargain at $1.56. Within a few months the stock tripled to a high of $5.38. In 2003, the stock skyrocketed to $39.30 or +2,419 percent!

The grandfather of modern turnaround (or contrary) investing is Sir John Templeton. In 1939, just after World War II started, Templeton called his broker and gave him a very unusual buy order. He instructed the broker to buy 100 shares of every stock on the NYSE and Amex that was selling for $1 or less. When his broker called back to confirm that he had bought all the stocks that were $1 or under, he mentioned that, of course, he didn't buy any stocks that were bankrupt. Templeton startled his broker by insisting that he also purchase the bankrupt stocks that were under $1.

In all, Templeton bought 105 stocks, 35 of which were bankrupt. After about four years, he sold those stocks for more than $40,000 or almost four times his original investment. Why did he buy the stocks? Templeton believed that the United States would eventually enter World War II and that would spur the economy and cause his 105 stocks to appreciate in value.

The stocks were extremely cheap, yet the companies had to be of high quality to meet the listing requirements for the NYSE and Amex. Templeton correctly assumed those stocks had good potential to turn around. Because of their low stock prices, they could easily have greater percentage moves, which would far outpace the higher-priced stocks.

While I don't recommend taking the chances that John Templeton did, he became one of the most famous and successful money managers in the world. In 1992, he sold the Templeton Funds, worth roughly $80 billion, to the Franklin Group, in a deal that netted him more than $900 million!

WHAT IS A TURNAROUND STOCK?

A formerly high-priced, successful stock that has experienced hard times, causing a drastic plunge in its stock price meets the first qualification for a turnaround candidate. However, as the name indicates, it also needs to overcome its severe problems and show the potential to resume being a successful company. Companies that survive bankruptcy are considered turnaround stocks, but many companies can be turnaround stocks without entering bankruptcy. In fact companies in bankruptcy are especially risky, as the struggling company can decide to issue new shares of stock to its debtors and the common shareholders sometimes are left with nothing. Kmart recently employed that tactic when it emerged from bankruptcy. It issued new shares of stock and common shareholders found their old shares worthless.

Typically, a turnaround stock has been promoted to an unrealistically high price with the expectation of higher profits due perhaps to a new product, service or acquisition. When it becomes apparent that the profits have not materialized or that the new acquisition, product or service is not going to be as successful as predicted, the stock price takes a nosedive. The price keeps falling, eventually becoming only a fraction of its high price. While the stock was very overpriced at its high, it may be extremely under-priced at its low.

Aspect Telecommunications - A Turnaround Stock

In August 1998, telecommunications stocks were hot, and Aspect Telecommunications (NASDAQ – ASPT) was one of the stars. Aspect was on most major buy lists, and momentum buyers were purchasing shares at $38. Nine months later, Aspect plunged to $6.44 and those momentum buyers lost over 75 percent of their investment.

While the price plunge was bad news for the momentum investors, it signaled a potential bargain for *The CHEAP Investor*. I analyzed the company and liked what I saw. The company did have problems as it shifted its focus from telecommunications equipment to becoming a leading supplier of enterprise software and solutions.

On the positive side, Aspect had excellent products, a solid balance sheet with almost $200 million in cash ($4 per share) and a book value of $5.23 per share. In February 1999 a director purchased 372,000 shares at $7 for a $2.6 million investment in the company. I recommended the stock in the April 1999 issue at $6.44. Over the next year the stock not only turned around, it soared to a high of $68! Investors who purchased 1,000 shares for $6,440 saw their investment skyrocket to a high of $68,000!

THE HUGE PROFIT POTENTIAL OF TURNAROUNDS

A quality turnaround stock has the potential to soar. One major advantage of a turnaround stock compared to other low-priced stocks is that it was previously at a much higher price and many analysts already know the stock. Name recognition (for either the company or its products) can make it easier for the stock to move up a second time.

Pre-Paid Legal Services, Inc. (NYSE - PPD) underwrites and markets legal expense plans primarily through direct mail and credit card billings. It is a good example of a turnaround stock. In the early 1990s, PrePaid Legal was a high flyer, selling for over $16 per share. Then the company experienced some hard times and the stock price plunged. In October 1994, the stock price was tremendously undervalued at $1.31, so I recommended it in *The CHEAP Investor*.

By 2000, Pre-Paid Legal's stock price had shot up to $49 per share (+3,640 percent), where it was on the buy lists of many major brokerage firms. The ability to recognize profit potential and, therefore, buy a quality stock at a low turnaround price is what separates the smart investors from the Wall Street followers.

Investing in a Quality Stock in a Depressed Industry

In a variation on the same theme, you can make money in depressed industries. Of course, the smart investor won't invest in just any stock. He analyzes companies involved in that industry, searching for one that has good growth potential. That way the investor has the opportunity to make a profit as the quality company responds to the normal upward fluctuation when the industry makes a comeback.

For example, the waste management industry has always experienced fluctuations. In the 1980s, waste stocks soared because the media convinced us we were running out of space for landfills and soon would be up to our necks in our own garbage. That prediction didn't materialize because recycling was introduced. According to recent statistics, recycling has been responsible for cutting the amount of waste going to landfills by almost 50 percent. The day of reckoning when there is nowhere else to put our garbage has been delayed. In fact, recycling has worked so well that instead of landfill prices soaring as predicted, they started to plunge because of competition. Consequently, stocks connected with the waste handling industry started to plunge as many companies lost money.

The October 1994 issue of *The CHEAP Investor* concentrated on environmental and waste management stocks, because they were selling at, or near, their 52-week low prices. The issue recommended four stocks, which I believed were great buys with excellent growth and profit potential.

Allied Waste (NASDAQ NMS - AWIN) at $3.25
American Waste (NYSE - AW) at $1.68
Kimmins Environmental (NYSE - KVN) at $1.50
Republic Waste (NASDAQ NMS - RWIN) at $3.00

The stocks didn't do much until the first quarter of 1995 when Wayne Huizenga of Blockbuster Video stepped into the picture. Huizenga purchased Republic Waste and indicated he was going to expand the company by acquiring smaller competitors. In response to this announcement Allied, American, and Kimmins soared; and Republic's stock exploded.

Investors who had the foresight to invest in those four quality companies, when the waste management industry was depressed, and held onto them for several months while they didn't move, were greatly rewarded.

Allied Waste jumped from $3.25 to $16.25 or +400 percent.
American Waste shot up from $1.68 to $5.63 or +235 percent.
Kimmins Environmental soared from $1.50 to $6.38 or +325 percent.
Republic Waste skyrocketed from $3.00 to $88.50 or +2,850 percent!

In fact, Republic Waste (now called Republic Industries) was one of the most successful stocks of the 1990s.

The Contrarian Approach

Individuals who invest in turnaround stocks or depressed industries are known as *contrarians.* As the name implies, this investment philosophy calls for investing contrary to what most investors and Wall Street are doing. The contrarian opinion is that if everyone is certain something will happen, it won't. It is the art of thinking for yourself, not succumbing to the influence of the crowd. This strategy works in just about any market because human nature is the same everywhere.

Most investors wait until they see mass buying before purchasing the stock themselves. Likewise, they wait until they see mass selling before they get out. (And they wonder why they can't make money in the stock market!) J. Paul Getty expressed this contrarian logic in his book, *How To Be Rich,* when he wrote that an investor should "buy when everyone else is selling and hold until everyone else is buying. This is more than a catchy slogan. It is the very essence of successful investment and accumulating wealth."

I use the contrarian approach when looking for stocks to recommend in my newsletter. *The CHEAP Investor* was the only newsletter I am aware of that recommended Republic Waste at $3.00. At that price, most brokerage firms were advising to sell the stock for a tax loss. However when it set new records for its price, you can be sure it was on the buy lists of most analysts. Won't they ever learn? It's Buy Low, Sell High!

IDENTIFYING AND SELECTING A QUALITY TURNAROUND

How do you discover the few turnaround stocks that have the potential for good profits? It takes research.

Locating Turnaround Stocks

The easiest way to find possible turnaround companies is to check *The Wall Street Journal, Investor's Business Daily or Barron's.* Look through the stock listings for a large spread between the 52-week high and low prices. Locating a stock with a high of $53 and a low of $2.75 indicates that something drastic has happened to the company. It will take further research to determine what it was and if the company has possibilities.

Another way to locate turnaround candidates is to follow the biggest percentage losers for the NYSE. (At least in the beginning I advise that you restrict yourself to NYSE-listed stocks since they are the largest, most profitable and well-known companies.)

I like to follow the percentage-losers' column because some of the best turnarounds started out being listed in this column when their prices plunged. You can also review the weekly, monthly and year-end percentage losers that are listed in *Barron's.* Some very well known companies have been listed in the percentage-losers' column. Another area you may want to check is the earnings reports that are listed on a daily basis in *The Wall Street Journal.*

Look for companies that have produced a profit after suffering previous losses. Over a period of time, you can accumulate a list of stocks that may be turnarounds, and you'll become familiar with their names and how their stocks trade. The next step involves research to weed out the bad stocks and find those select few that contain the elements for a tremendous stock-price move.

What to Look For in a Turnaround Stock

In November 1998, I researched Summit Technology (NASDAQ - BEAM). Summit is a leading developer, manufacturer and marketer of ophthalmic laser systems designed to correct common vision disorders such as nearsightedness, farsightedness and astigmatism.

In January 1996, Summit was a hot stock trading at $38 per share. Then Summit fell on hard times and its stock plunged to $4. After carefully analyzing Summit, I thought it was a good buy at $4 since the company had a great balance sheet with $83 million ($2.70 per share) in cash and investments. The company reported increasing sales and earnings. Over the next year and a half, Summit soared 600 percent before being bought out.

Most investors, including many brokers, choose turnaround stocks strictly by price. While this is an important factor, it is not the only one. I like companies that have established, well-known products, sales over $100 million and a stock price at 10 to 20 percent of its previous high price.

The most important element is the company's balance sheet. When a stock's price has plunged, it's typically due to unexpected, severe losses. These create negative cash flow, high inventory and large write-offs. It can take months or several years for the company to correct the problems that caused the losses and turn around its balance sheet. I like to buy a stock that has increased its cash flow and cash position, lowered its inventories and posted a profitable quarter.

I prefer to wait for the release of the positive figures rather than buying earlier when the company's management projects that it will produce a profitable quarter. I developed this tactic from experience when many projected profitable quarters never materialized.

In addition, the profits must come from continuing operations, not from tax credits or extraordinary credits. If the company is profitable only because of a big tax credit or an extraordinary credit from selling a division, it really hasn't experienced the turnaround. Its continuing operations will be the final factor in determining whether or not the company maintains its profitability.

Quarterdeck Office Systems, Inc., a well-known manufacturer of business and communications software, is another example of a turnaround stock recommendation. In the early 1990s, Quarterdeck was a Wall Street favorite selling at $27 per share. Then the company experienced a reversal in fortunes.

As the stock price plunged to $2 at the end of 1992, most brokerage firms recommended selling for a tax loss. I was intrigued by Quarterdeck's potential at that extremely low price and recommended it several times between the $2 to $3 level.

The Company continued its turnaround, and in 1995, Quarterdeck was one of the first software companies to introduce Internet communications software. The stock soared. By mid 1996, Quarterdeck was a high flyer again and back on the Wall Street buy lists at $39.50! The stock was bought out a couple years later at $0.50 per share, so it's important to take those profits when you have them!

TURNAROUNDS TO AVOID

Not all turnaround stocks are good investments. It is important to know which situations to avoid so that you don't lose money. Probably only about 5 percent of turnaround stocks are excellent candidates with good profit potential.

There will always be exceptions to the rule, but on the whole, if a company has any of the following negative factors, its chances of being a successful turnaround stock are severely limited.

Companies in Industries that are Extremely Capital Intensive

It is hard enough for a company to turn around its sales and earnings, create assets and working capital and lower its debt; but when it is in an industry that requires a lot of capital, this can be too much to handle. For example, if the company is in the entertainment, high-technology, real estate or pharmaceutical industries, where a large amount of working capital may be needed, and it can't obtain necessary capital through sales, it may be forced to issue more shares of securities or go further into debt. Either way, shareholder value is negatively affected.

I discovered a good example of this when I recommended Wessex Corporation several years ago at $2.50. The company managed many healthcare facilities in the southeastern part of the United States. When I recommended Wessex, it had just returned to profitability with a good increase in sales and earnings. The stock price did move up to $4.50 after the recommendation. However, Wessex posted a loss the following quarter and continued to raise necessary capital by going further and further into debt. That eventually caused the stock price to fall. The last time I saw Wessex's stock, it was selling for pennies.

The entertainment industry takes a great deal of capital to produce films. Orion Films was a major name in the motion-picture industry and its stock was a Wall Street favorite. However, most of its films didn't return enough to offset the company's huge debt. Even its tremendous hit, *Silence of the Lambs,* which grossed over $250 million, (an unheard of amount at that time) could not save it from bankruptcy.

Companies in the real estate and high-technology industries also need huge amounts of working capital. In most cases, their stock prices are several times the companies' book value. In particular, the book value of real estate companies can be greatly exaggerated.

Pharmaceutical companies invest tremendous sums on research and development and then still need to spend years testing their drugs before they obtain Food and Drug Administration (FDA) approval to sell their product to the public. Often a company will run out of money before it obtains FDA approval to market the drug and generate income.

Companies That Have an Extremely Large Debt

Many times, the stocks that plunge are ones with debt so massive that they can no longer make the payments. Not only does the company have to turn around its sales and earnings; it has to placate its many creditors. Since the company's common shares may be its only real asset when its debt is restructured, management may decide to issue additional shares to its creditors. Issuing a large number of shares severely dilutes the shareholder value as shown below.

Income Statement	Before Additional Shares	After Additional Shares
Revenues	$25,000,000	$25,000,000
Net Income	2,000,000	2,000,000
Net Income per Share	.20	.10
Shares Outstanding	10 Million	20 Million

Even worse, management could decide to totally restructure the company by issuing new shares. If this happens, the old common shares become worthless. Companies such as Continental Airlines, Ames Department Stores, Wang Labs and Emerson Radio resorted to this strategy to decrease debt. It's amazing that they can wipe out their current common shareholders, issue new shares in a restructured company and continue to do business. It certainly doesn't seem fair to the common shareholders who suddenly find that their investment has no value.

Companies That Offer High Percentage Dividends

This is a trap that catches many unsuspecting blue chip investors. They get caught when they look for low-priced stocks paying high-percentage dividends. They don't realize that most of the time the dividend percentage is inflated because the stock suffered losses and its price plunged. The dividend percentage (which is based on the previous dividend when the company was making more money) moves up in response to the lower price, giving a very false impression.

Many times, the investors find a high-percentage dividend and don't research the stock to see whether it has the cash to pay the dividend. If its stock price fell because of huge losses and debt, that could prevent the company from paying any further dividends. When the company suspends or discontinues its dividend, the stock price can plunge even further, and the investor has lost all around.

Companies Affected by Foreign Currency

Two types of companies fall into this category. The first is a company that purchases all its products from foreign countries. In the early 1990s, with the rapid fluctuation of the U.S. dollar, companies experienced huge losses just because the U.S. dollar's value declined.

The second type of company to bypass is one that sells the majority of its products to foreign countries and is paid in foreign currency. The fluctuation in the value of the U.S. dollar can severely impact the company's revenues and threaten its profits.

Companies That Are Recommended as Hot Tips

Don't take anyone else's word that a turnaround (or for that matter, any stock) is a great investment without doing your own research. If you are going to invest your hard-earned cash, it is worth the effort to analyze its annual report, 10-K and 10-Q reports. These reports can all be found on the Internet or you can call the company and ask it to mail a copy to you.

TAKE YOUR PROFITS

If you carefully research your investment candidates to find the one with the best potential and patiently wait for a low buying price, your profit can be enormous. I've watched stock after stock quickly double, triple, quadruple or more. However, make sure you take some of your profits off the table. You do not want to wind up like Quarterdeck's shareholders who saw their stock skyrocket from $2 to $38 only to be bought out months later at $0.50.

Chapter

┌─────────┐
│   │
│   8   │
│   │
└─────────┘

Mastering Stocks
in Bankruptcy

The term *bankruptcy* is so negative that most investors, brokerage firms and analysts don't even consider a company in bankruptcy as an investment. For this reason investing in bankrupt companies is almost universally ignored by the media. In 1986, I wrote *Successful Investing in Companies in Bankruptcy*. Even though the book has been out of print for many years, I still get calls from interested investors who are looking for good reference material on the subject. I'm including a chapter on stocks in bankruptcy for those investors.

Several years ago, one of the most well known names in retailing, Montgomery Wards, announced that it was filing bankruptcy, liquidating its assets and laying off its 25,000-employee workforce. This news must have been depressing for one of the largest and most successful financial corporations, General Electric Credit Corporation, which had well over $1 billion invested in Wards. The fact that a powerful corporation like General Electric Credit Corporation lost money on its investment in Wards illustrates that investing in bankruptcies can be very risky.

While they are speculative, companies in bankruptcy can offer great investment potential. If you are confused about the bankruptcy process, don't feel lonely. To the average person, bankruptcy means liquidating all of a company's assets and going out of business. Bankruptcy can mean that; however, Chapter 11 of the Bankruptcy Law offers an alternative to liquidation through the reorganization of the company. Sure, the company has major problems, but under Chapter 11 it is protected from its creditors while it reorganizes and conducts business; and it may very well survive that difficult period of time.

In fact, a company that experienced one of the largest percentage gains during the 1980s was Envirodyne Industries, a Chicago company that was selling for $0.25 in 1981 when it was in Chapter 11. It successfully reorganized, and years later it was bought out for $80 per share (taking into consideration a two-for-one stock split). That's an incredible gain of almost 319 times the original $0.25 investment!

The CHEAP Investor didn't do quite that well, for the newsletter recommended Envirodyne in October 1984, when it was at $2.81. When the former management group of Beatrice, Inc. bought Envirodyne at $80, my subscribers had a potential profit of 2,747 percent! It turned out to be a poor investment for Beatrice, as the stock price fell over the next several years, and in January 1996, I again recommended Envirodyne at $3.38. Two years later, the stock was again bought out, this time for $8.50 per share.

Six other Chapter 11 companies that increased by several hundred percent from their original *CHEAP Investor* recommendation prices are Charter Company, Storage Technology, AM International, Lionel Corporation, Wickes Companies and Emerson Radio.

The potential is there. The investor just needs to understand the bankruptcy process and how to analyze companies in Chapter 11. Investors can make a substantial profit by investing in companies in Chapter 11 because as soon as Wall Street even hears the rumor that a company is on the verge of entering Chapter 11, it panics. The stock price plunges as everyone bails out, and many times the price falls well below the true value of the company. After carefully analyzing the company to determine if it will be a survivor, the smart investor doesn't let this opportunity escape. He can purchase stock worth much more for just a fraction of the price that investors were recently paying for it.

Several companies have reorganized under Chapter 11 and emerged to become prosperous, vital enterprises. On the other side of the coin, many companies don't survive Chapter 11. Sometimes there are just too many negative factors, and after all is said and done, the company still goes into liquidation.

The list in Figure 8.1 shows companies that succeeded or failed in Chapter 11. Some of the failures are well-known names. That is why it is imperative to understand the bankruptcy process and thoroughly analyze the company before you invest.

Figure 8.1 Chapter 11 Companies

Successes	Failures
Emerson Radio	Montgomery Ward
Chicago-Milwaukee Railroad	Diamond Reo Motors
Envirodyne Industries	E. J. Korvettes
Storage Technology	Osborne Computer
Toys R Us	Sambo's Restaurants
Wickes Companies, Inc.	W. T Grant Company

BANKRUPTCY (CHAPTER 11) – AN OVERVIEW

To fully understand Chapter 11, you must first learn what bankruptcy encompasses. Bankruptcy is defined as "the state of insolvency of a person or corporation." Very simply, it is the inability of a person or company to pay its debts. The Bankruptcy Law was designed to accomplish two main objectives:

1. Protect the debtor (company filing bankruptcy) against any frivolous suits by creditors (companies or individuals who are owed money), especially when the debtor is still able to recover

2. Provide a fair means for distribution of a debtor's assets among all creditors. The bankruptcy process establishes priorities among creditors and prohibits the debtor from favoring one creditor over another.

The bankruptcy code contains several chapters. However, there are only two that apply to companies. Companies that suffer severe financial difficulties have a choice of liquidating (Chapter 7) or reorganizing (Chapter 11). Chapter 7 involves selling all the company's assets and distributing the monies received from the sale to creditors. The big disadvantage of Chapter 7 for the creditors is that they usually receive only a small percentage of the money owed them. Common shareholders may receive only a few cents per dollar value of the share or nothing at all.

The best alternative to liquidation for a company, its creditors and shareholders is filing for Chapter 11 to restructure the company's debts. Chapter 11 is the financial restructuring of a company after it has filed for protection from its creditors while it works out a plan to repay its overdue debt. The company normally files a reorganization plan within 120 days, and its debts are usually frozen for up to three years until the plan is approved. The aim of reorganization is to allow the company to continue operations while it negotiates with creditors and to eventually return the company to financial health.

If the plan fails, the company may be liquidated (Chapter 7) and its assets sold to pay the claims of creditors and shareholders. However, if the company succeeds, the creditors should be able to get most of the money owed them. In many cases, creditors have been very pleased with the settlements from large companies that entered Chapter 11.

LOCATING COMPANIES IN CHAPTER 11

Companies in Chapter 11 used to be listed in your local newspaper, *The Wall Street Journal, Investor's Business Daily* or *Barron's*. That's no longer true. In 2003, the Exchanges became more aggressive in delisting Chapter 11 stocks to the OTC Bulletin Board. Now it takes more research to develop a list of potential bankruptcy stocks.

The Internet has helped to fill this gap. A good resource for a list of stocks in bankruptcy is www.bankruptcydata.com. You can also scan the business headlines for major companies that are near to, or filing for, Chapter 11. When a company files for Chapter 11, its stock symbol normally changes by adding a Q before the symbol.

After compiling a list of companies in Chapter 11, your next step is to obtain information about them, so that you can determine which ones may be good investments. The Internet can provide a lot of information about the stocks. Yahoo's http://finance.yahoo.com is a great resource for company information and SEC filings. Check the company's own Website or sites that concentrate on bankruptcy stocks. You can also contact the company and request its annual and quarterly reports. Those reports can provide good background information. Another great informational source is a copy of the reorganization plan that the company usually issues within three to six months after filing for Chapter 11. You can obtain a copy of the plan by calling or writing the company.

Certain types of companies have generally proven to be good investments when they emerge from Chapter 11. There are always exceptions to the rule, but by looking for the following fundamentals, you can pare your list to a more manageable number of companies for in-depth research.

Companies with Huge Sales

Experience has taught me that the best type of Chapter 11 company is one with annual sales of at least $500 million. Any time a company enters Chapter 11, there is a chance that it will fail and be liquidated. However, a company with sales over $500 million obviously has been around for a while and usually has a large number of assets. It has a greater chance of surviving because the easiest and quickest way for a company to get turned around is to sell some of its assets to obtain the necessary capital to continue operations and/or to pay creditors.

On the other hand, a company that has only $50 million in sales and a $40-million debt, for example, is going to be hard-pressed to reorganize, pay its debts and still have enough capital to operate. The investor should definitely avoid any company that has more debts than sales. The chance that a company with sales of $400 million and a debt of $900 million will survive is practically zero.

Companies Listed on the NYSE

The New York Stock Exchange (NYSE) has the most stringent requirements for membership. If a company has been successful in the past (which a listing on the NYSE indicates), the chances are greater that it will have the ability and resources to be successful again. NYSE-listed stocks tend to have sales in excess of $300 million and are generally well known on Wall Street. This is a tremendous asset.

Often, a company on the NYSE will be delisted when it enters Chapter 11, so do some research to discover if it was originally listed on that exchange. (Checking a copy of *The Wall Street Journal* or *Barron's* from a month or so prior to the company entering Chapter 11 should show whether or not it was on the NYSE.)

Companies That Are Former "Darlings" of Wall Street

Another good candidate for successful reorganization under Chapter 11 is a former "darling" or Wall Street favorite. Many companies that had a stock price of $50 to $100 or more and were listed on the NYSE, are great investment choices because they are already well known.

Another advantage of a former Wall Street darling is that in most cases, some brokers will continue to trade the stock. Therefore, the company will have at least a limited following that should help push the price upward when it emerges from Chapter 11. Companies that did not interest Wall Street before they entered Chapter 11 probably would not be able to generate much excitement when they emerge from Chapter 11.

One Wall Street darling was Storage Technology (NYSE – STK). The stock, which sold as high as $40.38, was a leader in the computer data storage industry. A few years later, the company filed for Chapter 11 and traded as low as $1. When Storage Technology emerged from Chapter 11, it sold as low as $2, but quickly jumped to the $7 level because of its Wall Street following and its history of previous success. The stock really took off in 1998 and traded as high as $100 before splitting two for one.

Companies with Widely Known Names or Products

The most difficult hurdle for a new company is becoming known to the public and Wall Street. A company that does not have a known product has an extra deterrent to surviving reorganization because it still has to sell its product. If a company's product is well known, that asset could make the difference between reorganization and liquidation.

Lionel Corporation is an excellent example. Years ago I recommended Lionel at $3.25 when it was ready to emerge from Chapter 11. Less than two years later, the stock was $14. Lionel's biggest asset was its name recognition. Almost everyone had a Lionel train when they were young, or knew someone who did. Once Lionel streamlined its operations and sold off unprofitable divisions, its product sales were enough to ensure the company's success at that time.

SELECTING BANKRUPTCIES
WITH THE MOST POTENTIAL

Once you eliminate the obviously poor Chapter 11 candidates, there are several characteristics to look for to determine the company with the best chance of survival. Companies that address their problems by changing management, creating a workable reorganization and restructuring to return to profitability have the best investment potential.

Companies That Change Management

Poor management usually causes the downfall of many companies. No matter how good a company's products, if they are not marketed effectively and the company is not run efficiently, it will eventually lose money and may be forced into Chapter 11. If the income statement is not turned around, the company will be forced to liquidate to pay its debts.

Hiring a new CEO, who often brings his own management team, can be an important factor in the survival of a company. There are teams who specialize in turning around companies in or near Chapter 11, and if the team has a record of successfully reorganizing other companies, that's a big bonus. Because the new CEO brings his own people, this destroys all the old political alliances and allows the new team to measure products, divisions and employees on performance instead of clout. The ability to impartially cut out the deadwood and sell unprofitable assets is imperative to a company's survival.

Another consideration is the way the new management team is compensated for its work. If the team is paid a small salary but receives a large bonus and/or stock incentives for positive results, it will strive harder to turn the company around. This is because the team has a piece of the action and is being paid in direct proportion to the well-being of the company.

Companies That Become Profitable

A major component of successful investment in a Chapter 11 company, is to follow the company's income statement until it shows a profit. Even if a company has several of the previously mentioned criteria, its chances of surviving are very slim if it does not recover enough to show a profit. It is imperative to analyze the company's current income statement, which you can find in its latest quarterly report. Take a look at the example in Figure 8.2.

Figure 8.2 Sample of a Current Income Statement

	2003	2002
Sales	$175,360,000	$112,470,000
Income Continuing Operations	2,371,000	(820,000)
Income Discontinued Operations	716,000	(513,000)
Extraordinary Item Tax Credit	394,000	---
Net Income (Loss)	3,481,000	(1,333,000)
Income Continuing Operations per Share	.14	(.05)
Income Discontinued Operations per Share	.04	(.03)
Extraordinary Item per Share	.02	---
Net Income (Loss) per Share	.21	(.08)
Shares Outstanding	16,652,551	16,510,741

To better analyze the turnaround of a company's income statement, you need to look at the following information:

Sales (or Revenues) are the monetary payments received in exchange for goods or services, or from other sources such as rents, investments, etc. Don't be too concerned about a decrease in sales. In most cases, unprofitable subsidiaries have been sold, and this would cause the sales to decline.

Income from Continuing Operations is one of the most important areas to check on a Chapter 11 company's income statement. It is vital because these operations have survived and will become the basis for the company's sales and earnings. Check the figures to determine whether or not the continuing operations have increased their income over the previous year. An increase is a positive sign that a company is on the road to recovery.

Income from Discontinued Operations is a nonrecurring item that appears on the income statement to show a one-time income from a product or division that was sold or is being discontinued.

Extraordinary Item Tax Credit is a nonrecurring credit that offers a direct dollar-for-dollar reduction in tax liability. When a company loses money, that loss becomes a positive factor once the company regains profitability. Since the loss is deducted from taxable income, the company pays less tax.

Example: In the early 80s, Chrysler experienced tremendous losses. Then Lee Iacocca took control and slowly but surely turned the company around. When Chrysler became profitable in the late 80s, those losses came back on the income statement as a tax credit (or tax loss carry-forward) and were deducted from taxable income. Approximately 30 to 50 percent of Chrysler's net income resulted from those tax credits. Therefore, a large amount of tax credits (losses) can be a big asset when a company returns to profitability.

Net Income or Loss is the final profit or loss after all costs, expenses and taxes have been deducted. Net income may be misleading because it may contain profits from the sale of divisions or tax credits.

Per Share items are calculated by dividing the continuing operations, net income, etc., by the number of shares outstanding. This is an important metric, used to compare any increase or decrease from the previous year.

Shares Outstanding is the total number of shares issued. When comparing net income per share or income continuing operations per share with the previous year's figures, always make sure the shares-outstanding figure is approximately the same. Otherwise, comparing the per-share figures from one period to the next will be of little value.

Many times companies in Chapter 11 satisfy part of their debts by issuing more common shares. In Figure 8.2 the number of shares is just about the same. However, if the company issued an additional 30 million shares to satisfy its debt (which is not uncommon for a Chapter 11 company), then the per-share comparisons would be misleading, as is shown below.

Figure 8.3 Income Statement after Issuing a Large Number of Shares

	2003	2002
Sales	$175,360,000	$112,470,000
Income Continuing Operations	2,371,000	(820,000)
Income Discontinued Operations	716,000	(513,000)
Extraordinary Item Tax Credit	394,000	---
Net Income (Loss)	3,481,000	(1,333,000)
Income Continuing Operations per Share	.05	(.05)
Income Discontinued Operations per Share	.02	(.03)
Extraordinary Item per Share	.01	---
Net Income (Loss) per Share	.07	(.08)
Shares Outstanding	46,652,551	16,510,741

Note that the per-share items for fiscal 2003 have dropped drastically from Figure 8.2. By issuing such a large number of shares, the company has greatly diluted the value of its current shares. Dilution of share value should be considered when analyzing any investment.

Companies That Enter a Prepackaged Chapter 11

There's been a trend toward using a prepackaged Chapter 11 filing which is usually positive for a company. A company that is short of cash usually uses this strategy. The company negotiates with its major creditors and/or lenders to design a reorganization plan before entering Chapter 11. This type of Chapter 11 filing is successful because the company is generally sound, with reasonable debt, but lacks an adequate line of credit to continue its business. Filing Chapter 11 gives the company breathing room and the cash infusion it needs to turn around.

NYSE-listed Jamesway Corporation, which operates a chain of over 100 discount department stores in the East, is a good example. Jamesway's problem wasn't debt. In fact, in February 1993 it renegotiated its bank debt to extend a line of credit through 1996 to remodel its stores. Jamesway ran into problems when it ran short of cash to pay its suppliers for merchandise to stock the stores. Suppliers stopped shipping, and Jamesway entered a Catch-22 situation. As it wasn't able to obtain as much merchandise to sell, it had even less money to restock its shelves. The company was in a spiral that it had to escape, or it would die.

Jamesway negotiated a $75 million unsecured debtor-in-possession financing plan with CIT Group/Business Credit Corp. In July 1993, the company entered Chapter 11 and received the line of credit that would ensure the cash that Jamesway needed to restock. I analyzed Jamesway's situation and saw the filing of Chapter 11 to be a positive factor. I recommended it at $0.56 and the stock shot up to $1.38 in two weeks.

Companies that enter Chapter 11 using a pre-packaged bankruptcy usually emerge from Chapter 11 six to twelve months after entering. The prepackaged Chapter 11 plan usually details how the common shareholders will be treated. Since common stock is unsecured, several companies have left their common shareholders with nothing. Needless to say investors will want to carefully read the plan to avoid that situation.

Companies with a Confirmed Reorganization Plan

The strategy to satisfy the creditors of a company in Chapter 11 is called the reorganization plan. It usually is a compromise between the Chapter 11 company and the creditors and may involve full or partial payment of debts in cash, securities or other financial incentives.

It is important to read the reorganization plan to determine if a company intends to issue many more shares of its securities to pay off its debts. If so, those new shares will dilute the value of the stock, and the company may decide to use a reverse stock split as a "quick fix" to increase the stock price. I believe that a reverse stock split is very hazardous to the shareholders' wealth. Do not invest in a company that is planning to execute a reverse stock split.   If you already own stock, consider selling it.

A company usually files a reorganization plan about 120 days after going into Chapter 11 and normally has to amend it at least a few times over the next two to three years. The goal is to confirm the plan of reorganization, which means that two-thirds of the creditors and a majority of the claims in a class agree to the plan. If the bankruptcy judge approves the confirmed plan of reorganization, the plan binds all creditors, and the company can emerge from bankruptcy.

During reorganization the debtor and representatives for the creditors have periodic meetings. Each creditor representative tries to increase the amount of distribution that his group will receive, while the debtor tries to encourage a plan that will allow it to emerge as a successful, reorganized company with adequate funds to continue operations. Needless to say, a lot of discussing and compromising occurs before any plan is confirmed. If no agreement can be reached, the company may still end up in liquidation (Chapter 7).

A Chapter 11 company that has a confirmed plan of reorganization has passed a very important hurdle. The time element is important, too. One of the biggest mistakes a company can make is to come out of Chapter 11 too soon. Most successful companies stay in Chapter 11 for up to three years to take full advantage of the reorganization period.

I have noticed that some companies in Chapter 11 experience a quick price jump when the reorganization plan is approved. For example, Johns Mansville was selling for around $2, and when the reorganization plan was approved, the stock jumped by about 75 percent over the next couple of weeks.

TRENDS IN BANKRUPTCIES

Because the public is so willing to sue over almost anything and the courts are awarding huge settlements, many companies find themselves in dire financial straits because of lawsuits resulting from marketing a defective product or a product found to cause problems that show up years after it was used. This situation has caused some companies to seek the protection from creditors offered by Chapter 11 even though, according to their income statements, they don't really need to be reorganized.

On October 5, 2000, Owens Corning (OTCBB – QWENQ) filed for reorganization under Chapter 11 bankruptcy protection. The Company took this action in order to address the growing demands on its cash flow resulting from its multi-billion dollar asbestos liability. The lawsuits were filed against its product Kaylo®, a high temperature insulation containing asbestos that was sold decades ago. The Chapter 11 filing enabled Owens Corning to refocus on operating its business and serving its customers.

Lawsuits such as this have been the death knell for many companies in the asbestos industry. So far, almost 100 companies have been forced to close their doors, eliminating over 100,000 jobs. Class action lawsuits have also decimated companies in the tobacco, food, supplement, and pharmaceutical industries.

In the early 90s, class action lawsuits hit companies that manufactured breast implants. Silicone from leaky implants was blamed for a variety of ailments. Cooper Companies (NYSE – COO), which had an implant division, plunged from $30 to $0.30 because of such lawsuits. Luckily, Cooper was diversified, had huge assets and a good management plan, which helped it survive that assault. Cooper restructured and turned around. Over the next ten years, the Company's stock soared from $0.30 to $80 (considering stock splits). Years later, research showed that silicone did not cause many of the problems that the class action lawsuits had claimed.

Extremely high wages from labor contracts have been attacked by creative use of Chapter 11. Continental Airlines (NYSE – CAL) filed for Chapter 11 in the mid-1980s, when its costs became too high to compete in its marketplace. By filing Chapter 11, the Company no longer was required to honor contracts, including those with labor unions. Many unions consider this tactic to be union busting. However, it allowed Continental to renegotiate lower wages for its employees. In return, the employees were able to keep their jobs instead of having to seek new ones because the business was forced to liquidate.

It is ironic that after Continental cut its labor costs (in addition to many other cuts), it not only survived bankruptcy but became a profitable major airline for several years until it again filed Chapter 11 in November 1990. More than a decade later, Continental is a successful international airline.

The 9/11 terrorist attacks wreaked havoc with the airline industry. As terrified tourists decided to stay close to home, several airlines were forced into bankruptcy. In 2003, United Airlines (OTCBB – UALAQ) filed bankruptcy after its stock plummeted from over $100 to $0.40. American Airlines (NYSE – AMR) also plunged to $1.25 and was on the verge of bankruptcy. Last minute concessions from employees saved the day and over the next couple of months the stock soared to $12.

Why did American Airlines recover while United was forced into bankruptcy? The big difference was the Companies' balance sheets. United had a deficit book value of ($4 billion), while American had a positive book value of $2 billion. That money saved American from having to resort to bankruptcy. It will be interesting to see what happens to United. Personally, I think the Company will survive, but the common shareholders most likely will be left with nothing.

Management Sellout to Creditors

A disturbing trend has recently gained momentum. Chapter 11 was instituted to protect a company from its creditors while it negotiated its debt and tried to successfully reorganize. Smart management teams utilize Chapter 11's protection and the threat of liquidation to negotiate the debt down to $0.20 to $0.30 on the dollar. This strategy protects the shareholder's equity and allows the company to emerge from reorganization with more assets.

However, some management-team members seem to be more concerned with satisfying creditors to avoid liquidation and losing their jobs rather than safeguarding the shareholder's investment value and the company's health. Instead of negotiating to reduce the debt, occasionally they will actually pay the whole debt and give interest to the creditors. The only way they can accomplish this is to offer the creditors shares in the company, which means issuing millions of new shares. The new shares severely dilute the stock value and shareholder's equity. In many cases, the original shareholders received less than 5 percent of the newly restructured company. If you see this happening to a stock you own, sell it immediately.

Common Shareholders are Not Secured Creditors

Chapter 11 is also being used in another way, to shaft common shareholders. In some instances, when the company is reorganized, new stock is issued to only the creditors and management. Meanwhile, the common shareholders are left out in the cold because they are unsecured creditors. This tactic has been used by Continental Airlines, Continental Bank, Ames Department Stores, Wang Labs, Emerson Radio and Kmart.

Emerson Radio's (Amex – MSN) reorganization had a unique twist. Instead of signing an agreement with its lenders for a portion of the debt, the company borrowed from its largest shareholder. It used that money to buy back its debt from its secured creditors at $0.30 on the dollar. Then Emerson formed a restructured company issuing new stock. The new management group invested $30 million in Emerson and received 30 million shares.

Unfortunately, the company wasn't so kind to its common shareholders. They did not receive any of the new shares and the old shares they had were worthless. Emerson's management did give common shareholders the right to buy shares based on a percentage of what they had been stuck with at $1 per share. Shareholders who invested once again in Emerson saw their investment triple to $3 within six months.

Though we didn't like Emerson's shafting of its common shareholders during reorganization, the company did redeem itself. I recommended the stock several times in 1998 and 1999 at $0.44 to $0.50. In 2003, Emerson soared to $8.00!

Just recently, Kmart (NASDAQ – KMRT) entered Chapter 11 and wiped out its common shareholders. The company issued new shares, making the old shares held by its common shareholders worthless. Kmart emerged from Chapter 11 and went public again at $16. The stock is now at $25. I think more companies will resort to this tactic, since some high profile stocks have used this strategy very successfully.

Figure 8.4 Largest Bankruptcies in the last Twenty Years

Company Name	Bankruptcy Date	Assets
WorldCom, Inc.	7/21/02	103,900,000,000
Enron	12/2/01	63,392,000,000
Conseco, Inc.	12/18/02	61,392,000,000
Texaco, Inc.	4/12/87	35,892,000,000
Financial Corp. of America	9/9/88	33,864,000,000
Global Crossing Ltd.	1/28/02	30,185,000,000
UAL Corp. (United Airline's parent)	12/9/02	25,197,000,000
Adelphia Communications Corp.	6/25/02	21,499,480,000
Pacific Gas & Electric Co.	4/6/01	21,470,000,000
Mcorp	3/31/89	20,228,000,000
First Executive Corp.	5/13/91	15,193,000,000
Gibraltar Financial Corp.	2/8/90	15,011,000,000
Kmart Corp.	1/22/02	14,600,000,000
FINOVA Group, Inc.	3/7/01	14,050,000,000
Home Fed. Corp.	10/22/92	13,885,000,000
Southeast Banking Corp.	9/20/91	13,390,000,000
NTL, Inc.	5/8/02	13,026,100,000
Reliance Group Holdings, Inc.	6/12/01	12,598,000,000
Imperial Corp. of America	2/28/90	12,263,000,000
Federal-Mogul Corp.	10/1/01	10,150,000,000

It's amazing how many companies file bankruptcy. In the first quarter of 2003, almost 2,500 companies filed Chapter 11. The 20 largest bankruptcies since 1980 are listed in figure 8.4.

As I write this chapter, there is a lot of concern about the bankruptcy laws. WorldCom/MCI (Pink Sheets – WCOEQ), the largest company to ever file bankruptcy, is set to emerge from Chapter 11. Competitors are complaining that WorldCom/MCI ran up huge debt (in some cases owed to those competitors), and is now able to exit bankruptcy with a clean slate. Competitors who suffered through the bad times but did not file for bankruptcy are claiming it's unfair. Don't be surprised if some changes are made in the Chapter 11 laws.

Investing in companies in bankruptcy has changed over the past few years. It has become more speculative and takes a lot of research; but it can be profitable. For those who can stand the risk, the best strategy is to invest in several of the very cheap bankruptcy stocks at $0.10 to $0.50. If and when you get a good move, take your profit! Because of the time and amount of research required to be successful, I think there are better *CHEAP* stock investments available in the market today.

Chapter

Mastering New Issues

When forming a new company, many entrepreneurs plan to eventually take it public by offering shares of its stock to the public. This is the entrepreneur's opportunity to become rich, powerful and well known. Imagine how satisfying it would be to open up the morning paper to check the price of *your* company. Achieving the American Dream, going public, is a great opportunity for the entrepreneur, the company, its employees and its investors.

THE NEW ISSUE PROCESS

To better understand what you are getting when you purchase a new issue, let's start at the beginning of founding a company to look at the aspects of going public and issuing stock.

Entrepreneur's Dream

Most companies begin with an idea for a new product or service or a better way of offering an existing product or service. The founder (or entrepreneur) establishes the company to fulfill that idea. The founder usually has enough capital or is able to borrow enough from family and friends to get going. However, when additional capital is needed to expand research and development, production or marketing, the company may find itself in the Catch-22 situation of finding that most banks aren't interested in lending money to small companies when they need it. So the company offers a new issue of stock to obtain the needed capital.

The Business Plan

One of the most important documents a company will prepare is its business plan. In essence, the plan is a map that the company intends to follow to successfully bring its product or service to the market. The business plan must have an appreciation of present realities and must indicate a logical course of action, including the capital and resources needed. It should take into account the overall industry, trends, potential problems and economic direction. It should also include company characteristics, its balance sheet, management experience and specific company goals.

The business plan is vital because it is the first document that any bank, venture-capital firm, investment banker or underwriter will request when a company is seeking to raise capital. Let's assume that Elgin Watch Company has achieved good sales and earnings by selling its watches for six years in the Midwest; however, it wants to expand its market to the West Coast. An aggressive expansion of its market will cost Elgin Watch Company a tremendous initial investment. The company doesn't have enough capital for the expansion, so it decides to raise the capital through a public offering of a percentage of its stock. This is an important decision, and the advantages and disadvantages of going public should be carefully analyzed.

As explained in Chapter 4, going public is one of the easier ways, and sometimes the only way, to get needed capital. The public offering puts a value on the company and can be used as an incentive to attract and motivate key personnel. Once the company has public shares, it can sell more shares when additional capital is needed.

However, offering a new issue does have a negative side; issuing the stock and keeping the shareholders up to date are expensive undertakings. Once public, the company (except for pink-sheet stocks) is obligated to file reports with the SEC, which greatly increases paperwork and legal expenses (as much as $100,000 per year). The company loses privacy, for now the shareholders have a right to know everything that can affect the company's success. It also loses control over some major decisions, such as mergers, and there is increased pressure for better sales and earnings.

Once the Elgin Watch Company has carefully weighed both the pros and cons and decides to go public, it must locate a brokerage firm that is willing to underwrite its new issue stock.

The Underwriter

An underwriter is a brokerage firm that acts as the intermediary between the company issuing new securities and the investing public. The underwriter (or investment banker) either by itself or as part of a syndicate (two or more underwriters) agrees to purchase a new issue of securities from a company and distribute it to the investors. A major consideration of the new issue is what percent of the company should be given to the public for the amount of capital the company wants to raise. Let's say that the underwriter and Elgin Watch Company decide that they need to give up 50 percent of the company to raise $5 million for the market-expansion program.

The company and the underwriter sign an agreement that represents the underwriter's commitment to purchase the securities, and Elgin Watch Company agrees to pay all expenses incurred in preparing the stock issue for resale, including the costs of registration with the SEC and preparing, printing and distributing the prospectus. The underwriter generally takes a commission of 10 percent plus expenses for selling the stock.

Structuring the Deal

The underwriter will determine how much money the company can raise and at what price the shares should sell. Once a value has been given to the new issue, there are many combinations of shares and prices. For example, if $5 million is to be raised, it can be offered at several different prices. (See figure 9.1.)

The underwriter, using expertise gained from previous new issue offerings, determines the price that it believes will be most advantageous for selling the new issue. The price of the stock then will define how many shares will be offered.

Figure 9.1 New Issue Share/Price Combinations

Number of Shares	Price	Amount Raised
500,000	$10.00	$5,000,000
1,000,000	5.00	5,000,000
2,000,000	2.50	5,000,000
5,000,000	1.00	5,000,000

Registering with the Securities and Exchange Commission (SEC)

All companies can use the Form S-1 to register their securities offerings with the SEC. If a company qualifies as a "small business issuer" it can use Form SB1 to offer up to $10 million worth of securities in any 12-month period.

An investor who wants to investigate a company, or an individual connected with the company, can use the SEC library at any of the regional or branch offices. SEC offices are located in Atlanta, Boston, Chicago, Denver, Fort Worth, Los Angeles, Miami, New York, Philadelphia, Salt Lake City, San Francisco, Seattle and Washington, D.C. You can contact the SEC's main office in Washington D.C. at U.S. Securities and Exchange Commission, 450 Fifth Street, NW, Washington,

D.C. 20549-0304. The telephone is (202) 942-2950. The SEC's Internet address is www.sec.gov. You can also check the stock with the North American Securities Administrators Association (NASAA) office in your state. You can find the location of that office by accessing the Internet address www.nasaa.org/nasaa/ abtnasaa/find_regulator.html. For more information contact North American Securities Administrators Association, 10 "G" Street, N.E., Suite 710, Washington, D.C. 20002. The telephone is (202) 737-0900. NASAA's Internet address is www.nasaa.org.

Warning – Most investors mistakenly believe that the SEC protects them from new issue frauds. While the SEC reviews the registration statement of a company, it *does not have the authority* to pass judgment on the worth of the securities of that particular offering.

Many investors assume that if a new issue is registered with the SEC, the SEC checks out the company and gives it an approval. This assumption is false. The SEC has no *power to prohibit an offering* on the basis that it considers the investment opportunity to be a poor risk. No matter how speculative the investment, no matter how poor the offering, it complies with federal law if all required facts are disclosed. In essence, as long as a company fills out the registration forms correctly, the SEC must allow the company to sell its securities.

Red Herring

After the registration statement is filed with the SEC, a waiting period begins before the final approval of the registration. The SEC normally takes at least 30 days to review the filing. However, the waiting period could be much longer if the SEC has received many registrations. There usually is a rush of filings at the end of each quarter, which can further delay the review.

In the interim the underwriter can give prospective investors the preliminary prospectus or *red herring* (so named for the red ink on the cover page of the brochure). The red herring offers financial details about the issue or statutory prospectus; however, parts of the document may be changed before the final prospectus is issued.

Prospectus

Once the company has satisfied all SEC requirements and made any changes required by the SEC, it can then print the final prospectus. This document needs to be given to investors before the offer or sale of securities can be made. I recommend that all investors carefully read the prospectus before making a decision on the investment. SEC law states that investors in a new issue must be sent a prospectus and must have time to read it before purchasing the security.

No matter how good the broker makes the company sound, take time to read about it. You may save yourself a lot of money and aggravation.

Filing in Individual States

After the company files its registration form to offer a new issue with the SEC, the underwriter must apply directly to each state in which the underwriter desires to sell shares. Virtually all states have a form of the blue-sky law, which was written to protect the citizens of that state from securities frauds.

The term *blue sky* originated from a famous 1915 case in which Justice McKenna asserted that a particular stock offering had as much value as a "patch of blue sky". The blue-sky law requires sellers of new stock issues to register their offerings and provide financial details on each issue so investors can base their judgments on relevant data.

However, the blue-sky laws of some states are so restrictive that almost all new issues fail to meet their stringent requirements. How does this affect you? An underwriter cannot legally sell shares of a new issue to an investor unless that investor is a resident of a state in which that new issue is registered. If you live in a state with very restrictive blue-sky laws, it may be virtually impossible for you to invest in any new issue before it goes public. That doesn't make a lot of sense when you consider that, once the stock goes public, it becomes available to everyone, even those who were restricted from purchasing it a few weeks before.

TYPES OF NEW ISSUE OFFERINGS

When an underwriter buys a new issue from a company, it must decide how confident it is that the new issue will sell. Based on that confidence, the firm will either underwrite the new issue as a *firm-commitment* or *best-effort* offering.

The optimal type of new issue offering is a firm commitment, which means the underwriter is putting its reputation and company on the line. The underwriter is committing to purchase *all* the new issue securities for sale to its customers. If all the shares are not sold, the underwriter is obligated to pay the company and hold the unsold shares in its own account.

> **Example:** If an underwriter gives Elgin Watch Company a firm commitment for its new issue offering of 1 million shares at $5 each, the underwriter is guaranteeing that the company will receive $5 million (minus commissions and expenses) whether it sells all the shares or not.

The second and more speculative type of new issue offering is called a best-effort offering. This is an agreement between the underwriter and the company that the underwriter will act as an agency to sell the shares, promising to apply its best effort in selling the new issue to its customers. However, no guarantee is given that the offering will succeed. A minimum and maximum number of shares is usually listed in the prospectus.

For the new issue offering to go through, the minimum number of shares must be sold, or all monies will be returned to the investors. This means that the company issuing the securities doesn't get its needed capital and has spent tens of thousands of dollars in legal fees, printing costs and time expended for nothing. Even though this sounds pretty grim, the vast majority of best-effort new issue offerings do succeed.

> **Example:** The underwriter has set a minimum of 2 million shares and a maximum of 3.5 million shares at $1 for Elgin Watch Company. If the underwriter is able to sell 2 million or more shares, the new issue will proceed. If the underwriter is unsuccessful in selling the 2-million share minimum, the investors will receive a refund.

When the investor buys new issue stock from the underwriter, his money is put into an escrow account until the new issue actually goes public and starts trading. Because the underwriter has 90 days in which to sell the new issue and can get a 90-day extension, the investor's money can be tied up for six months or more.

Why buy from the underwriter? Because in a bull market, the purchase price of the new issue usually shoots up immediately after it goes public and is offered on the secondary market. Be aware that in an average or bear market, the new issue price may very well go down shortly after it goes public.

UNDERWRITER SYNDICATION AND SUPPORT OF THE NEW ISSUE

In most instances, when an underwriter contracts to take a company public, the syndication department recruits other brokerage firms to market part of the new issue. (See Figure 9.2.)

Working together, the brokers in the selling group market the shares to their customers and, once it goes public, continue to support the new issue with investors who will buy the stock in the aftermarket (the secondary market). Doing so creates an orderly and fair market for the stock.

The selling group continues to promote and support the new issue after it goes public by offering the stock to more customers when the stock is on the secondary market. Because of the number and diversity of the brokerage firms involved, more investors become aware of the stock, and the group of potential investors in the company vastly increases.

Figure 9.2 Underwriter Syndication of a New Issue

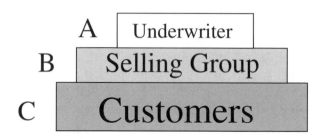

A. The company sells its new issue to an underwriter and the underwriter syndicates a portion, perhaps up to 60 percent, of the new issue to other brokerage firms, which is known as the underwriters' syndicate or selling group for the new issue.
B. The brokerage firms in the selling group create an interest for the new issue by bringing it to the attention of their customers.
C. The customers invest in the stock, creating a market for the new issue.

That's the situation I like to see. However, when a new issue is a penny stock, which usually has only one underwriter, the scenario changes. (See Figure 9.3.) Because the underwriter does not syndicate the new issue, it can better control the price of the stock.

Figure 9.3 Penny-Stock New Issues

A. The company sells its new issue to a penny-stock underwriter, but the underwriter keeps the whole new issue and creates an interest in the stock through its clients.
B. Far fewer customers invest in the stock, creating a smaller market for the new issue.

In the second scenario, the market has been artificially created, and the stock price may plunge when the underwriter moves on to its next new issue. Major brokerage firms usually derive a small percentage of their total sales from new issues. However, some penny firms may obtain the majority of their total sales from underwriting and selling new issues. The more brokers involved in a new issue, the better the chance for good support of the stock in the aftermarket.

An important new issue term is *quiet period.* This usually is a 90-day period after the prospectus' effective date when the company is not allowed to release any new information. For the purpose of maintaining an orderly aftermarket, the SEC requires the quiet period to regulate public statements by the company.

If the company has some very good news to release during the quiet period, such as a major new contract or agreement, it can petition the SEC for permission to release the information. If the SEC approves the petition, the company can add a sticker to the front page of the prospectus that contains a brief outline of the news.

From the legal point of view, *a broker, newsletter or newspaper can only report information that is included in the prospectus when promoting a company offering a new issue.* However, this rule is often violated; especially by penny-stock brokers. They may tell their customers about information, which is not contained in the prospectus, such as future plans, contracts or agreements that will be completed in the near future. Sometimes the future plans or contracts materialize, sometimes they don't. Believe only what is written in the prospectus and you won't be disappointed.

HOW TO EASILY READ A NEW ISSUE PROSPECTUS

Whenever you are looking to purchase a new issue, the first step you should take is to read the new issue prospectus. If a broker calls you with an "unbelievable investment opportunity" in a new issue, don't just take that broker's word. Insist that the broker send you a prospectus. By law, a broker is not allowed to sell you a new issue before you read the prospectus, but an unscrupulous broker may "forget" that you haven't seen one.

The *prospectus* is a formal, written offer to sell securities. It contains information that a potential investor needs in order to make an informed investment decision. The prospectus describes the company's business history, operations, its management's background, financial data, pending litigation (if any) and plans, including the use of the proceeds from the new issue.

Once you receive the prospectus, don't be intimidated by all the legal terminology. Reading a prospectus, especially for the first time, can be a real chore. Use the highlights that follow to quickly learn what the new issue has to offer, and determine if you want to invest in it. Every prospectus is slightly different, so the items mentioned here might not be found in the prospectus you are reading. Take a look at our sample prospectus title page for Elgin Watch Company in Figure 9.4 .

- *Section A*. This section lists the total number of shares or units (combination of shares and warrants) that the company is offering for sale to the public.

- *Section B*. This section provides the name of the company that is offering shares or units to the public.

- *Section C*. If the company is offering an unit, this section tells what the unit consists of. It also gives details of the value of the shares and the warrants. It sets the warrant's exercise price and expiration date.

- *Section D*. While the SEC has required that the company follow the correct procedure in filing for the public offering, the SEC is not guaranteeing the accuracy of the information contained in the prospectus. In other words, the SEC does not investigate to determine the quality of the investment. This statement is included in every prospectus.

- *Section E*. An SEC-required summary of the risk factors is listed. This statement is included in every prospectus.

- *Section F*. This section indicates whether the issue is a Firm-Commitment or Best-Efforts offering.

- *Section G*. The table shows the price of the new issue ($5 per unit or $5,000,000), the commission the underwriter will receive for selling each unit (10 percent or $500,000) and the actual amount of proceeds the company will receive from each unit (90 percent or $4,500,000).

- *Section H*. The name and address of the underwriter who is offering shares of the new issue before it goes public is listed in this section. You can purchase the new issue only from that underwriter, or other members in the syndicate of underwriters, who are bringing the company public. Once the new issue goes public, you can purchase the stock from any broker.

- *Section I*. This section shows the effective date (the date when a registered offering may be sold to the public). The underwriter normally has 90 days from the effective date to sell the new issue. If the underwriter runs into difficulties selling the security, it may obtain a 90-day extension to complete the offering.

Figure 9.4 Sample Prospectus for Elgin Watch Company

A

B   # 1,000,000 Units
C   # Elgin Watch Company

Each unit consisting of One Share of Common Stock and One Warrant
to Purchase a Share of Common Stock

Elgin Watch Company (the "Company") is offering (the "offering") through WK Mathews as the representative (the "Representative") of the underwriters herein names (the "Underwriters".) 1,000,000 Units of the Company's securities. Each Unit consisting of one share of $.01 par value common stock ("Common Stock") and one redeemable common stock purchase warrant ("Warrant") at a purchase price of $5 per unit. The Common Stock and Warrants are separately transferable as of the date of the Prospectus. Each warrant is exercisable to purchase one share of Common Stock at $6.25 per share (125% of the Unit Price) for a period of two years from the date hereof and may be redeemed by the Company for $.01 per Warrant on 30 days' written notice to the Warrant holders if the closing price of the Common Stock on the NASDAQ SmallCaps Market is at least $7.50 (150% of the Unit Price) for 20 consecutive trading days, ending not earlier than five days before the Warrants are called for redemption. The Unit Price and Warrant exercise price have been determined by negotiations between the Company and the Representative and such prices are not necessarily related to the Company's financial condition, net worth or other established criteria of value. For a description of the factors considered in determining the Unit Price and the exercise price of the Warrants, see "Risk Factors" and "Underwriting"…

D   **THESE SECURITIES HAVE NOT BEEN APPROVED OR DISAPPROVED BY THE SECURITIES AND EXCHANGE COMMISSION, NOR HAS THE COMMISSION PASSED UPON THE ACCURACY OR ADEQUACY OF THIS PROSPECTUS. ANY REPRESENTATION TO THE CONTRARY IS A CRIMINAL OFFENSE.**

E   **The securities offered hereby involve a high degree of risk and substantial dilution and should be considered only by persons able to sustain a total loss of their investment. See "Risk Factors".**

The Units are offered on a "firm commitment" basis by the Underwriters,
F   subject to prior sale, when, as and if delivered to and accepted by the
Underwriters and subject to certain conditions…

G

	Price to Public	Underwriting Discounts and Commissions	Proceeds to Company
Per Unit	$5.00	$.50	$4.50
Total	$5,000,000	$500,000	4,500,000

W. K. MATHEWS SECURITIES, INC.
H   1000 N. MICHIGAN AVE.
CHICAGO, IL 60601
The date of this Prospectus is November 4, 2003

I

The first page of the prospectus tells quite a bit about the cost of the new issue security and where you can purchase it. Inside the prospectus, you will learn about the company, its products or services, its goals, its marketplace and competition, the quality of its management and other factors important to the success of the new issue.

After checking the first page of the prospectus, turn to the prospectus summary (usually near the front of the prospectus). The summary outlines the most important information in the prospectus. It contains information about the following:

- *The Company.* This section details the company's background, business and products or services offered.
- *The Offering.* The offering explains the number of shares or units being sold. If units are involved, it specifies what comprises each unit. If warrants are involved in the offering, the exercise price and expiration date are stipulated.
- *Shares Outstanding after the Offering.* This part indicates the total amount of shares that will be outstanding once the new issue is completed. To determine what percentage of the company is being given to the public, divide the number of shares offered by the total number of shares outstanding. I like to see a company give 35 to 60 percent of its ownership in a public offering.

  Example: If Elgin Watch Company has 10 million total shares outstanding and the offering is 5 million, the company is offering 50 percent of its ownership to the public.

- *Use of Proceeds.* This explains in detail how the company plans to spend the money raised by the new issue. Many times the proceeds are used to pay down long-term debt, for the development of new products or as working capital. Look for a specific plan to expand the company's product or service or, in the case of a company in the development stage, to bring its product to the market. The plan should state the amount of money to be spent at a specific time to implement the various stages of the strategy. If the prospectus is vague about how the capital will be utilized, stay away from that new issue.

  Hint: Avoid a new issue that plans to use the proceeds to repay loans from management. The new issue is being used to benefit the company's management rather than the company itself.

- *Proposed NASDAQ Symbol.* This is the company's stock symbol that will be used when the stock starts to trade. A smart company will plan ahead and obtain its NASDAQ stock symbol so that when it goes public, it can immediately be listed on the NASDAQ system, Many companies will try to select a stock symbol that relates to its business. For example, Elgin Watch Company may choose the symbol TIME for the common stock and TIMEW for the warrant.
- *Selected Financial Information.* This section lists information about the company's finances. It usually includes sales or revenues, net income and net income per share for the past three or more years. This area also lists the total assets, total current assets, total current liabilities and shareholder's equity.

By reading the prospectus summary, you should be able to decide if the company has a good chance of being successful. If after reading the summary, you still believe it is a good potential investment, you will want to check further by reading selected areas in the rest of the prospectus. Make sure that you read about:

- *The Management.* Review the management's background to see if the people possess the necessary experience and knowledge to be an asset to the company. If their background experience is in completely different areas from the company's business, be very careful. Check whether the chairperson of the board, president and vice-president are spending 100 percent of their time with the company. If key management personnel are not devoting themselves solely to that company, stay away. If they have headed one or more public companies that ended in bankruptcy, do not invest.

- *Litigation.* Be sure that the company is not involved in any major lawsuits that could seriously affect its business.

- *Management Compensation.* This section can help the potential investor determine if management is weakening the company with huge salaries. I would rather see salaries below average with bonus incentives paid when management achieves certain goals regarding increasing sales and earnings.

- *Risk Factors.* The prospectus is filled with bleak and discouraging disclaimers that are required by the SEC. While the SEC is trying to protect potential investors by making sure that they understand all the risks involved in buying a new issue, it can frighten investors away from a good investment. Once you have read a few prospectuses, you will recognize the disclaimers and take them into consideration without letting them discourage you from investing in a quality new issue.

MAKING AND LOSING MONEY IN NEW ISSUES

New issue securities can offer great profit potential if the investor researches before investing. Many poor new issue investments can be eliminated just by carefully reading the prospectus. Buy a new issue only *at the new issue price;* otherwise, you may end up paying an inflated price. The purchase price is a key factor that can determine whether or not you make a good profit. In a bull market, once the new issue goes public and is allowed to trade on the secondary market, the price normally skyrockets. Investors who were unable to purchase a stock at $1 at the new issue price may find themselves paying $2 for the same stock once it goes public.

Be aware that many new issues are very overpriced when compared to stocks that have traded for several years. Analyze the company as you would any other stock and purchase the new issue only if you would buy it at that price, if it were a common stock. Avoid new issues that do not raise at least $4 million. Even if the new issue is a company in the development stage, the $4 million will guarantee the stock a listing on NASDAQ. Always make sure the new issue will be listed at least on the NASDAQ system. If the company plans merely to be listed on the pink sheets, the Vancouver Stock Exchange or other foreign exchanges, *do not invest in it.*

Whether or not you can purchase a new issue is determined by your resident state. Several states have relaxed blue-sky laws, allowing investors to purchase most new issues. These states include Colorado, Florida, Illinois, Nevada, New Jersey, New York and Utah.

Some states are very restrictive about new issues. It is virtually impossible to purchase a speculative new issue if you reside in California, Pennsylvania, Texas or Wisconsin. Since blue-sky laws continue to change, you can learn about your state's laws by contacting your local state securities regulator office, which is usually located in the state capital. You can find a listing at www.nasaa.org/nasaa/abtnasaa/find_regulator.html.

I believe that the restrictive states are making a mistake. While protecting investors from poor investments, these states also keep investors from buying some great low-priced stocks. Often a $1 new issue will not meet the criteria of those states, and their citizens will be unable to purchase the new issue before it goes public. Once the stock goes public and receives the capital raised by the stock issue, it qualifies for listing in Standard & Poor's, which automatically allows the stock to be bought by residents in most states. However, by that time the stock price has already jumped from the $1 new issue price to $1.50, $1.75 or higher.

Over the years, I have recommended many new issues that have been great investments. One of my superstars is CarePlus a $1 new issue. CarePlus provides home health care services to the acutely ill patient. The company offers laboratory tests, pharmaceuticals, nutritional feeding through a vein or tube, anticancer drug administration, intravenous organic drug administration and rehabilitation therapy. At the time I recommended CarePlus I believed that home health care would expand tremendously, since it is much cheaper than hospitalization. The company didn't disappoint me. It traded as high as $22, which gave my subscribers a nice 2,100 percent return. Recently the company was bought out.

Once you have determined that a new issue is a good investment (i.e., a quality company at a low price) and have purchased the new issue, it is essential to monitor your stock very carefully. Many times a new issue will skyrocket and then, just as quickly, fall back. If you get a good profit (50 to 100 percent), *don't be afraid to take some of that profit.*

NEW ISSUE SCAMS

In the 80s and early 90s there were a large number of penny stock underwriters who would offer penny stock new issues selling at $0.01, $0.05 and $0.10. Penny new issues became very popular because the low price allowed investors to buy many shares. Those investors didn't realize that many underwriting firms would issue all the shares of the penny new issue to their clients, thus controlling the whole market for the stock. Many of the penny new issues would quickly run through their IPO (Initial Public Offering) money and then close their doors. Even though the stock only cost pennies per share, the investors who still had shares lost everything. The big money makers were the companies' owners and the underwriters.

Some of the infamous penny stock firms were Blinder Robinson, Stuart James and First Jersey Securities. Those firms are gone now, but the game continues. The strategies used to con unwary investors just change with the times. Today IPO promoters issue stock in many different areas. Unfortunately, the only investors who can get into the really hot new issues today are large clients of the brokerage firm. Usually small investors can only get into the less attractive new issues.

Smart investors avoid new issues of companies that take the back door to become public. Instead of filing with the SEC and contracting with an underwriter to issue the public offering of shares, the company will merge with a public "shell" corporation. A shell corporation is a reporting company listed on the OTC Bulletin Board or the Pink Sheets. The shell has no operations and little assets. It is either formed specifically to merge with another company that wants to go public or is the shell of a corporation that went bankrupt and is no longer in business.

A company looking to go public can merge with a shell quickly and cheaply. Usually it takes 30 to 60 days to merge, and the company avoids having to file with the SEC. However, the primary reason a company goes public is to raise capital. Merging with a shell usually offers little cash infusion. The company still needs capital and will have to do a secondary public offering issuing more shares and thus diluting shareholder value. If a stock hasn't been trading long, call the company and ask how it went public.

Make sure the new issue is registered with the SEC. Also avoid any IPO promoted on the Internet – especially one that comes to you by unsolicited e-mail. Avoid any new issue that is a self underwriting. If the new issue isn't underwritten by a brokerage firm, then there will be no support for the stock in the aftermarket. Always make sure you receive a complete prospectus and read it carefully before investing.

In 1999 and 2000 there were many hot Internet IPOs. The price would double and triple in the first day of trading. A few lucky investors took their profits, but most were buying at those inflated prices. In many cases that initial day of trading became the all-time high price and it went down from there.

If you like a new issue and it soars on the opening day, have patience. Many times the stock price will fall, and six to nine months later, the patient investor can purchase shares at 50 to 25 percent of its IPO price. Currently individual investors are better off investing in quality, low priced stocks than initial public offerings.

Chapter

$$\boxed{10}$$

Choosing the Best Broker for Your Needs

Brokerage firms have come a long way from the days when they strictly bought and sold stocks for their customers. Today most types of personal financial services are available through one kind of brokerage firm or another, including life insurance, real estate partnerships, mutual funds, financial planning and even checking accounts. Selecting the best broker for your needs takes a little planning and effort, but it could be one of the most important decisions you make.

You must first decide what kind of investor you are or would like to be, and where you plan to go with your trading. Are you a novice? Do you want investment advice from your broker, or would you prefer to pick your own investments? The answers to these questions will determine whether you need a broker who charges higher commissions, but offers investment advice, or just the least-expensive broker available to execute your investment trade.

FULL-SERVICE VERSUS DISCOUNT BROKERS

There are distinct differences between a full-service/financial planner, a discount broker and an Internet broker. The *full-service/financial planner broker* offers personal service. In the past few years the full service broker has had to adapt to a new ballgame. He has converted from buying and selling individual products for a set commission to managing individual portfolios. As commission fees plunged, full service firms geared their marketing toward managing $100,000+ portfolios for wealthy investors and small business owners. Today, many full service brokers spend their time satisfying the needs of experienced investors who want someone who can manage investment accounts, pension funds, 401Ks, etc. As a result the full service broker has moved away from the investor who only buys stocks, especially the beginning investor with limited capital. You can still find brokers who will help small investors, but they are getting fewer every day.

This movement away from the small investor has created a niche for the *discount broker*. A discount broker buys and sells stock for you at a lower commission rate. He generally does not recommend specific securities or strategies and may not offer individual investment counseling or financial planning. The discount broker won't inquire or care about your personal balance sheet. Since the broker receives a salary instead of part of the commission fee, he has no incentive to solicit your business to increase his paycheck.

With the passage of time, certain discount brokerage firms have begun to offer more and more services. Typically the more services that are offered, the higher the commissions charged to cover the cost of the additional services. Firms such as Charles Schwab offer many extra services, but they are near the higher end of the discount commission scale.

Many discount brokerage firms discriminate against CHEAP stocks by charging a higher commission fee for trades on stocks costing $1 or less. (Some firms even charge higher fees for stocks under $2.) I've seen several discount firms advertise a $25 flat fee for stock trades. However, the fees on lower priced stocks can be much higher, sometimes as much as $200-$300 per trade for several thousand shares of an extremely low-priced stock. Investors who buy large amounts of CHEAP stocks may do better using an *Internet broker*.

The number of Internet brokers soared as the growth of personal computers and the Internet revolutionized the industry. As more and more investors learned to research potential investments on line, they realized that buying and selling on line could save them big bucks. Internet brokerage firms charge a flat fee of $6 to $20 per transaction. Many of these firms offer the ability to punch in your buy or sell order over your home computer or touch-tone telephone. Internet brokers offer the least amount of services but charge the cheapest prices. This can add up dramatically when you consider the savings for both buying and selling the stock.

As an investor, you don't want to pay higher commissions for services you won't be using. However, if you are inexperienced, it may be well worth the additional cost to get a broker who will help you make wise investment decisions.

FINDING, KEEPING AND WORKING WITH A BROKER

Just as you would search for high quality and value in a new car or home, you also should shop around for a good broker. After all, you are going to trust the broker with your money, so you want to be sure that he is honest and will give you profitable advice and service.

Today many experienced investors have a full service brokerage firm that handles their retirement and pension accounts, a discount brokerage firm to manage their mutual funds and smaller stock accounts, and an Internet broker for buying and selling large amounts of low-priced stocks.

If you are very knowledgeable about the stock market and know exactly what you want to buy and sell, then you basically want an "order taker" who will execute your trades, and your main consideration will be commission. However, if you need more help in making wise investment decisions, you need more than an order taker. The following information will guide you in finding the right broker for your needs.

Locating the Right Broker for You

You must first decide what type of broker or brokers you need for your investments. Do you need advice on your investments? If so, a full-service broker should be your choice. If you know what you want to buy, a discount or even an Internet broker may be best for you.

Your next step is to find some good broker candidates. You can ask for referrals from friends, your tax accountant or professional acquaintances who are involved in the market, such as your banker. If you don't know anyone who can recommend a broker, you can refer to the list of brokerage firms (in Figures 10.1, 10.2 and 10.3) that have excellent reputations. If you live in a larger city, many of these firms will have a branch office that you can locate by looking in your local telephone directory. You can also look at brokerage firm advertisements in *Investor's Business Daily*, *Barron's*, the *Wall Street Journal*, *Smart Money* and other investment periodicals. The Internet is also a fast way to research various firms.

A Full-Service/Financial Planner Broker If you are calling a full-service broker, you'll want to inquire about the types of investments he specializes in. Indicate how much you want to invest and request that the broker send you several ideas.

As a courteous client, you should call to interview your broker candidate after the market is closed. That way you won't be depriving him of the opportunity to make a commission from another client who wants to buy or sell stock

Figure 10.1 Full-Service/ Financial Planner Brokerage Firms

American Express Financial Direct 800-658-4677 www.americanexpress/direct.com	**Morgan Stanley/Dean Witter** 800-584-6837 www.online,msdw.com
Dreyfus Brokerage Service 800-416-7113 www.edreyfus.com	**Oppenheimer & Co. Inc**. 800-999-6726 www.oppenheimer.com
A. G. Edwards & Sons, Inc. 314-955-3000 www.agedwards.com	**USB Paine Webber** 212-713-2000 www.painewebber.com
Merrill Lynch, Inc. 212-419-1000 www.merrilllynch.com	**Prudential Securities, Inc.** 212-214-1000 www.prusec.com
J. P. Morgan 212-483-2323 www.jpmorgan.com	**Smith Barney** 212-816-6000 www.smithbarney.com

If you are calling a full-service brokerage firm, you should realize that most firms have a "broker of the day", who takes calls from individuals who haven't asked for a specific broker. You'll need to ask that broker which investment areas he specializes in and discuss how much you have to invest. You can request that he send you some investment ideas for consideration.

Be careful of any broker who pushes you to buy immediately. You want service, not pressure, from a broker. Be aware that all full service brokerage firms require a minimum of $5,000 and sometimes $10,000 or more to open an account.

Once you have at least three broker candidates, interview and meet with each candidate to discuss his strategy for handling your account. The broker needs to know how much you expect to have available for investments and what type of investments interest you, so make these decisions before talking to the broker.

Don't be intimidated by an impressive office or a smooth sales pitch. Discuss your financial goals and investment capabilities completely with the broker. He should express interest in your financial status and your personal taste in investment strategies. To help you get started, here is a list of some questions that you can ask your broker candidate:

1. How long have you been in the securities industry? How long have you been with this brokerage firm? Where did you work before?

2. Are you a Certified Financial Planner (CFP)? (A CFP has completed a rigorous course of study and passed an exam to earn this title.)

3. Where do you get investment recommendations? Do you research them yourself or rely on others?

4. Do you have client references?

5. How many clients do you have? Are you readily accessible by telephone to handle my transactions?

6. What specifics do you look for before giving a buy or sell recommendation? What's your philosophy for profit taking?

7. How are the firm's commission fees figured? Are there any discounts? Are there any other charges for services or monthly fees?

8. What services does your brokerage firm offer? Does it have in-house personnel to research and analyze companies and market trends?

9. What's the financial condition of the brokerage firm? (Ask for the latest annual and quarterly reports.) Is it a member of any recognized national stock exchange?

10. What do the monthly customer statements include?

You're the only one who can judge whether the broker's services, investment guidance and commission fees are compatible with your own investment objectives. If you want to invest in stocks under $5 per share, make sure your broker is comfortable with buying low-priced stocks. Your goal is to find a broker who is honest, efficient, dependable, easy to reach and, most importantly, feels responsible about the capital you are investing.

A Discount or Internet Broker If you are an individual who makes your own investment decisions, you want to find an inexpensive brokerage firm. Because the brokers at discount firms basically are order takers, you'll be more interested in the commission schedule. Contact several firms to ask for information about opening an account.

They should send detailed literature explaining their services and commission fees. Comparing the information from each discount brokerage firm should give you the basis to make an intelligent decision as to which to use. Avoid firms that charge higher fees for low-priced stocks.

Figure 10.2 Discount Brokerage Firms

Accutrade 800-882-4887 www.accutrade.com	**Quick and Reilly, Inc.** 800-837-7220 www.quick-reilly.com
Brokerage America 877-265-1218 www.brokerageamerica.com	**Charles Schwab & Co.** 800-648-5300 www.schwab.com
Brown & Company 866-302-7696 www.brownco.com	**Muriel Siebert & Co.** 800-535-9652 www.msiebert.com
Fidelity Investments 800-544-7272 www.fid-inv.com	**Scottrade Securities** 800-619-7283 www.scottrade.com
My Discount Broker 888-882-5600 www.mydiscountbroker.com	**T. D. Waterhouse & Co.** 800-934-4448 www.tdwaterhouse.com

Consider having more than one broker. In fact, if you have only one broker, it's hard to gauge how well he is doing. Many investors employ two or more brokers whom they use for different investments. You also should consider using an Internet broker to execute your trades, when you know exactly what you want to buy. Contact a full-service broker for help in choosing other investments. (I believe that it is very inconsiderate for an investor to buy a full-service broker's investment recommendation from a discount brokerage firm to save commission fees. If your broker made the recommendation, you should buy the stock from him.)

Figure 10.3 Internet Brokerage Firms

Ameritrade Securities 888-723-8512 www.ameritrade.com	**My Track** 800-698-7225 www.mytrack.com
Ceres Securities 800-669-3900 www.ceres.com	**National Discount Securities** 800-888-3999 www.ndb.com
Datek Securities 718-435-7100 www.datek.com	**Net Investor** 800-638-4250 www.netinvestor.com
E*trade Securities 800-786-2575 www.etrade.com	**J. B. Oxford Securities** 800-782-1876 www.jboxford.com
First Trade 888-988-6168 www.firsttrade.com	**A. B. Watley** 888-229-2859 www.abwatley.com

Beware of the Unethical Broker

Brokers (and some brokerage firms) are just as susceptible to dishonesty and prone to mismanagement as are any other professionals who routinely handle large sums of money. It is easy for an unethical broker to take advantage of an inexperienced investor. In the past some brokers have promoted questionable stocks to their clients. Always make sure you research any stock that your broker recommends.

When you find a broker with whom you feel comfortable, you should check with your local branch of the NASD to make sure that no complaints or sanctions have been brought against him. Each state has its own securities regulator. You can find your regulator at the Website of the North American Securities Administrators Association at http://www.nasaa.org/nasaa/abtnasaa/find_regulator.html. You can also learn the disciplinary history of any brokerage firm and sales representative by calling the NASD's toll-free hotline at (800) 289-9999.

OPENING AN ACCOUNT

Before you make any transactions with your new broker, you will need to complete a new account form, which is required by the SEC. Figure 10.4 shows a sample form. While some of the questions may seem awfully nosy, they're for your protection. Your broker must know your financial situation to decide which types of investments would best fit your circumstances.

Just because you have confidence in your broker, you shouldn't ignore your investments. After all, mistakes can happen, especially in the hectic day-to-day rat race of a brokerage house. However, if the same mistake (or mistakes in general) keep occurring, you've found a bad broker and should terminate your relationship. Remember, the brokerage community is a free market, and you are at liberty to move from one broker to another as you please.

If you feel uncomfortable with your brokerage house or broker, don't feel guilty about taking your account elsewhere. Your financial future is at stake, and that comes first. Never stay with a broker if your relationship ceases to be potentially profitable.

Should you Take Possession of Your Stock Certificates?

For many years I advised investors to ask their brokerage firms to send stock certificates directly to them. Times have changed and physically holding on to your stock certificates is no longer necessary. In fact I expect the SEC eventually will eliminate stock certificates altogether.

Figure 10.4   Typical New Customer Account Application

New Account Application

Investment Objectives	☐ **Appreciation with Risk** ☐ **Income with Risk** ☐ **Income with Safety** ☐ **Speculative** ☐ **Tax Reduction**	

Enter the Legal Name and Mailing Address on the next 6 lines

☐ HOME Address

Prefix First Name	Middle Name Last Name	Suffix

☐ BUSINESS Address

Prefix First Name	Middle Name Last Name	Suffix

Street Address

Street Address

Street Address

City…or for international accounts, City, Country, etc.	State/City	Zip Code

Home Tel. No.	Business Tel. No.	Date of Birth

Employee of Person?	Employee Related?	Name of Employee and Relationship	U.S. Citizen?	If No, specify country of citizenship
☐ Yes ☐ No	☐ Yes ☐ No		☐ Yes ☐ No	

Employment	Employer's Name	Est. Annual Income	Years Employed
	Employer's Address		
	Nature of Business	Occupation	☐ RETIRED *(indicate former occupation and employer)*

Spouse	Spouse's Name	Spouse's Occupation	Spouse's Date of Birth
	Spouse's Employer	Address of Spouse's Employer	

References	Bank Name and Address	☐ Checking ☐ Check if verified ☐ Savings
	Does client have accounts with other brokerage firms? If YES, which firm? ☐ Yes ☐ No	If client or members of household have other accounts with us, give nos.

General	Marital Status ☐ Married ☐ Divorced ☐ Single ☐ Widowed	No. of Dependents	☐ Own Home ☐ Rent	Net Worth *(excl home)*	Net Liquid Assets

Tax	Federal Tax Bracket: % (Omission indicates voluntary refusal to supply)	Annual Income	Other Tax Consideration

Interested Party	Line 1
	Line 2
	Line 3

City…or for international accounts, City, Country, etc.	State/City	Zip Code

DISCRETIONARY AUTHORIZATION ☐ None ☐ Limited AE ☐ Limited 3ʳᵈ Party	If granted, Agent's Name and Address

Special Instructions:

Applicant Signature   Initial Deposit

X_____ $

Locating a good broker can be a time-consuming process, but the wise investor will make the effort to find an honest, knowledgeable broker with whom he feels comfortable. Because the average investor does not fully understand the risks involved in investments such as options, commodities, futures and penny stocks, his broker is obligated both ethically and legally to know the client and suggest investments suitable for the client's situation.

Your broker must be readily available for your calls. If he doesn't have time to take your orders during a regular day, imagine the type of service you would get during a market crisis. Remember; a broker will give his best clients the best service. If you are a small investor, you need a broker who will work hard to service your account, even if it is modest. Finding the best broker for your needs is a key element of wise investing.

Chapter

How and When to Buy Stocks

Attention! This is one of the most important chapters in this book. Read it carefully, because it is contrary to the process most investors use when deciding which stock to buy. Here's my radical approach: don't worry so much about the market, instead, spend more time searching for and analyzing your investment candidates.

It's hard to do because the financial media inundates us with information about market trends. Whether its CNBC, *The Wall Street Journal* or an Internet financial Website, a good portion of their time and space are spent announcing the closing prices of all the indexes and what they think the current fluctuation means. It's easy to get bogged down by all the numbers and forget that your main goal is to find a stock with profit potential.

HOW TO FIND STOCKS

Investors must train themselves to recognize opportunities. Very simply you need to view companies you run across every day with an eye toward investment. It could be an intriguing store you discover at the mall, a company you pass every day on your way to work or a catchy ad on TV that opens your eyes to the potential.

In January 2000, I was searching for buy recommendations for *The CHEAP Investor*. CarMax (NYSE – KMX), which was selling at $1.56, caught my eye. I was familiar with the company because I had driven by one of its huge used cars superstores in my neighborhood. I also noticed ads in the local newspaper and on the radio. "Wow, an investment candidate," I said to myself. "Time to start researching."

I called several friends. Had they visited CarMax? Did they like it? I got positive feedback from those who had visited the superstore. They liked the clean cars offered for a reasonable, non-negotiable price. The consensus was CarMax took the headache out of buying a car. With further research I discovered that CarMax was a spin-off from Circuit City (NYSE – CC), which was selling at $62 per share. I spoke to several analysts who didn't like CarMax. (They probably bought the stock when it was selling at $22 and now were selling for a huge loss.) Instead they recommended buying Circuit City.

Being contrary, I decided the time was right to recommend the stock in the newsletter. Once again, going against Wall Street worked beautifully. By mid 2002 the vast majority of the market was plunging. CarMax, however, broke $34 for a potential 2,079 percent profit! (By the way, Circuit City (that the analysts like so much) plunged to $6 from that $62 price. Who says the individual investor can't beat Wall Street at its own game?

Buying the right stock for the right price is the key to making a good profit. After investigating several stocks and determining that they are quality companies, the smart investor doesn't just enter a buy order at the market price. He takes the time to establish a target price near the 52-week low and waits for the stock to reach it.

HOW TO BUY STOCKS

After choosing the stock you want to buy, it is important to completely understand the process involved in purchasing stocks.

Buying Stock – Size does Matter

The amount of money you have to invest and the price of the stock will determine the number of shares you can buy. Depending on the size of your investment capital, you should consider diversifying by purchasing three or more stocks. (If you are starting out with only $1,000 to invest, you will want to use it all for one stock. If you have $10,000, you can easily diversify into two, three or four stocks.) I advise that you begin with smaller amounts until you are confident that you are investing wisely.

Always buy stock in a round lot, which is the standard trading unit for stocks and warrants. Round lots are sold by the hundreds. Therefore, you can purchase stocks in any multiple of 100 such as 100, 200, 300, 1,000, 1,200, etc. Any number of shares from 1 to 99 is considered an odd lot, and you will usually pay a higher commission. In most cases an investor buying an odd lot (say 75 shares) will end up paying an extra $0.10 to $0.15 per share when both buying and selling the stock. If you want to purchase 275 shares, this would be bought in a round lot of 200 shares and an odd lot of 75 shares. Because of the increased fees, I recommend buying only in round lots.

Since many brokerage firms now charge a flat fee, the cost to purchase 1,000 shares is usually the same as only 100. Therefore, I suggest purchasing 1,000 shares or more if your funds allow it.

Type of Buy Order

Once you determine which stock and the number of shares you want to buy, you must decide what price you are willing to pay. You can enter your purchase order a couple of different ways.

Market Order The vast majority of all stock orders are executed by *market order*. Very simply, you call your broker and authorize him to enter your order to buy at the best price available at the time your order reaches the floor of the stock exchange (in other words, at the market price). Market orders usually are given top priority on the communication systems of most brokers and can usually be executed in a few minutes. If you purchase your shares through an Internet broker, the transaction may only take a few seconds.

Limit Order Designating a specific purchase price for the stock is called a *limit order*. The limit order can be good for the day, the month or until executed or canceled. For example, you call your broker and learn that the stock price is $1.75, but you wanted to buy it at $1.25. You can enter a limit order specifying the $1.25 price that you are willing to pay for the stock. Because many stocks move up and down during the day, there's a good chance that your order at $1.25 will be filled. While the limit order can save you some of the purchase price, there is no guarantee that the stock will drop down to the price you have set, and you may miss buying into it. Of course, if you like the $1.75 price, but don't want to pay any more than that, you can also enter a limit order specifying $1.75.

HOW TO BUY THE RIGHT STOCK AT THE RIGHT PRICE

The price you pay for a stock directly affects how much profit you will eventually make. No matter how high quality a stock is, if it is currently selling near its high price, your chances of making a good profit are greatly reduced. Time and again momentum buyers have learned this lesson the hard way – smart investors buy a stock near its 52-week low price.

•   Rule 8   •
Buying a stock near its low price is key
to your profit.

Most stocks are cyclical and only a tremendously positive occurrence would cause the stock to move a good deal higher than its 52-week high. Unless something drastic happens to the company, its stock will typically move up near the 52-week high, gradually fall near the 52-week low and then start back up again.

Therefore, it is essential to set a target price near the stock's low price and wait for the stock to meet that price before purchasing it. You also want a stock that shows at least 100 percent spread between its 52-week high and low price; otherwise, the stock price may not move enough to make it a good investment. Trading volume is another important factor. I like to invest in stocks that trade at least 100,000 shares daily.

How do you determine the target price? Compare the 52-week high and low with the current price. For example, a stock is selling at $2 a share, and its 52-week high is $8.75. Its 52-week low is $1.13. You might set a target price at $1.50, which is about 25 percent below the current $2 price and near the 52-week low. If the stock falls to $1.50, you purchase it. When the stock moves back up to $2, instead of just breaking even, you are already ahead 33 percent.

Of course, there's no guarantee that the stock will go down to $1.50. However, I have found this technique to work about 70 percent of the time. When you are trying to buy a stock near the low point of its cycle, it is possible that the stock will go even lower after you purchase it. By setting a target price below its current price, you are at least partially protecting yourself. Buying your stock at the right price is a critical factor in maximizing your profits.

PATIENCE AND DISCIPLINE PAY

You've found a great little company that has good potential; your only problem is that its price is too high. Now comes the difficult part. You have to ignore that money burning a hole in your pocket and wait for the stock to fall to your target price. This takes a lot of discipline and patience, but it pays in the long run.

•   **Rule 9**   •
Patience can pay off profitably.

Sometimes I will follow a stock for a year or more before it hits the perfect combination of being a high-quality company with a low price. It takes discipline to wait for the right price, but this can make the difference between profits and losses.

Patience and discipline are certainly major factors in the difference between an average and an exceptional investor. One of the investment classes that I taught was a five-week course specializing in low-priced stocks. During the first class I asked my students not to buy any stocks until they finished the course and had a much greater understanding of how to invest wisely. By the fourth class, I would ask the students if they had followed my advice and resisted investing in all the stocks we discussed as examples. They didn't have to raise their hands; I could tell by the sheepish grins on their faces. In most cases at least half of the students didn't have the discipline to wait.

Too many investors hear a story about a "great stock" and have neither the patience nor the discipline to check it out. Instead, they rush to buy the stock "before it soars" and are greatly disappointed when the stock turns out to be a flop. How many times has someone told you about an unbelievable stock that is going to make you a lot of money if you invest? I know that I have been tempted by such stories. However, if I actually investigated the stock, it usually was a poor investment risk. Perhaps the main reason why boiler-room brokers are so successful selling penny stocks, commodities, futures, worthless oil and gas stocks and other scams is that they know the average investor has no patience. Rather than exercising a little discipline to analyze the stock, the foolish investor is talked into buying immediately because all he can see is the money he thinks he's going to make.

In my business I get calls each day from brokers and company officers telling me how wonderful their stocks are. I have learned to never let a good stock story overwhelm my discipline. I always analyze the stock before making any investment decision, which has saved me a great deal of trouble and money.

DOLLAR COST AVERAGING

Dollar cost averaging is among the simplest and oldest of all formula investment plans. It basically consists of investing a constant amount of money in stocks over a long period of time, regardless of the level of the stocks' prices. This technique allows an investor to realize profits as long as the stock price eventually moves up and the same dollar amount of investment continues to be purchased periodically.

For example, an individual has $4,000 to invest each year and buys $1,000 of a stock each quarter. As the stock price rises, fewer shares can be bought with the $1,000; and when the stock's price dips lower, more shares can be bought.

The example in Figure 11.1 shows a typical variation in a stock's price. For dollar cost averaging to work, two ingredients are necessary. First, the securities' price must be volatile, and it should be on an upward trend. Money cannot be made on a stock whose price shows a continuous downward trend. By diversifying your portfolio, you greatly reduce this danger.

Second, the investor must be willing and able to purchase securities of an equal dollar amount when stock prices are low as well as high. During a depression salaries may be cut, and the money available to follow the plan may be reduced or totally lacking at the very time when stock prices are at their lowest, and therefore, most-attractive level.

The success of dollar cost averaging hinges on being able to liquidate the portfolio when the securities' prices are high. The investor can increase profit potential by planning to liquidate the portfolio several years before it is needed. Thus, the investor can delay the final liquidation if a stock's price is too low.

Buying securities through a monthly investment plan is a type of dollar cost averaging. It is also a great type of forced savings plan. The periodic buying of mutual fund shares and regular contributions to a pension fund such as a 401K plan that invests in common stocks could also be classified as a type of dollar-cost-averaging program.

Figure 11.1 Typical Variation in a Stock's Price

Quarter	Amount Invested	Market Price	Shares Bought	Total Owned	Total Invested	Value
1	$1,000.00	$2.50	400	400	$1,000.00	$1,000.00
2	1,000.00	3.00	333	733	2,000.00	2,199.00
3	1,000.00	4.00	250	983	3,000.00	3,932.00
4	1,000.00	3.25	307	1,290	4,000.00	4,192.50
5	1,000.00	3.00	333	1,623	5,000.00	4,869.00
6	1,000.00	3.75	266	1,889	6,000.00	7,083.75
7	1,000.00	4.00	250	2,139	7,000.00	8,556.00
8	1,000.00	4.25	235	2,374	8,000.00	10,089.50

HOW TO AVERAGE DOWN

A major difficulty in purchasing stocks is that you have no way of knowing what low price the stock will hit before it turns around and starts its upward cycle. Unless you own a crystal ball which reveals that information, all you can do is make an educated guess and hope you are right. However, there is a strategy that can prove useful.

When you purchase a stock, consider buying only half as many shares. Then if the price falls, you can buy more shares at the lower price and lower your *break-even point.* Your break-even point is the average price paid for all shares of stock. (If you bought 1,000 shares at $1.75, your break-even point would be $1.75.) Once the stock price moves above the break-even point, you are making a profit. Of course, before buying any more stock, first determine that nothing serious has happened to the company, causing the price to fall. After reanalyzing the company and concluding that it is only a normal price fluctuation, then and only then, should you consider averaging down.

For example, if you had $3,500 and wanted to purchase 2,000 shares of Global Marine (NYSE – GLM) at $1.75 per share, instead of buying all 2,000 shares at once, you purchase just 1,000 shares at $1.75. This leaves some available cash to purchase more shares if the stock price falls. This scenario happened after one of my Global Marine recommendations. You could have purchased the first 1,000 shares at $1.75, leaving $1,750 for further investment.

Sure enough, the stock fell to $1.25, and if you bought at that price, your $1,750 would have purchased 1,400 additional shares. Figure 11.2 shows how that would affect your break-even point. By lowering your break-even point to $1.45, when the stock moves back up to $1.75, you already have made a profit of 20 percent!

Figure 11.2 Averaging-Down Example

1,000 shares at $1.75 = $1,750	
1,400 shares at $1.25 = $1,750	$3,500 ÷2,400 shares = $1.45 average price
2,400 shares $3,500	

Most investors make the mistake of putting all their cash into a stock so they don't have anything available to average down when the opportunity presents itself. Even if the investor does have some accessible cash, he will usually just invest in another stock rather than take advantage of averaging down and lowering the break-even point.

By the way, after Global Marine backed off to $1.25, it turned around and shot up to $5.75 a share. If you had purchased the original 2,000 shares at $1.75, they would have been worth $11,500. You would have had an $8,000 profit or +228 percent. However, if you had averaged down, you would own 2,400 shares for a value of $13,800. Your profit would have been $10,300 or +294 percent!

Averaging down is the opposite of what most Wall Street experts recommend. They prefer to see their clients average up. Using the same example, let's say you bought 1,000 shares of Global Marine at $1.75.

The stock moved down to $1.25 and then started back up. It passed $1.75, and when it reached $4, your broker recommended buying more, so your $1,750 balance would purchase 438 additional shares. You now have 1,438 shares, and if they were sold at the $5.75 price, your total would be $8,269. Your profit would have been $4,769 or 136 percent. That is quite a bit less than what you could have made averaging down. I advise that you only average down. Never average up on your investments.

TAKING ADVANTAGE OF THE NEXT BULL MARKET

Many small investors miss bull markets because they follow the crowd. Shortly after starting my newsletter, in the fall of 1981, many stocks were extremely undervalued. However, most small investors hesitated to get into the market at that time. Instead they waited until late 1986 or early 1987 to jump on the bandwagon, at the height of the media hype, when everyone was talking about how much money could be made in stocks. Consequently, those investors bought stocks at extremely high prices, assuming that the stocks would continue to move even higher. Unfortunately, October 19, 1987 dashed those hopes when the market plunged more than 508 points.

When I wrote *Winning BIG with Bargain Stocks* in 1991, my economic models indicated a strong market led by small stocks. Since then many analysts and the media in general have mis-forecast this market due to the much publicized downsizing of major corporations. They are just beginning to realize that the true job creators in today's economy are the small- to mid-sized companies, not the Fortune 100 companies. For this reason, small stocks have far outpaced the blue chips over the last several years.

Twice in the 1990s the market hit an extremely low point where most investors were too nervous to buy. The few brave souls wise enough to grab some great bargains reaped huge rewards when the market rebounded.

During times of volatile markets we found some great companies at low prices. Stocks like PrePaid Legal skyrocketed from our $1.31 recommendation to $44 or +3,259 percent. Republic Industries soared 2,850 percent from $3 to $88.50. Arrow Electronics hit $72, up 1,820 percent from our $3.75 buy price. Access Healthcare shot from $3.36 to $65 or +1,835 percent. GRC International jumped 1,400 percent when it moved from $3 to $45.

By the late 90s the market fell once again. This time the situation was different. The old DOW blue chips were being replaced with computer and Internet companies such as Microsoft, Gateway, Dell, Sun Microsystems, Yahoo and America Online. The Internet also changed the way many investors bought and sold stocks. Instead of calling a full service broker, investors traded on the Web. Commission prices for buying and selling stock plunged to unbelievably low levels.

We found several winners during those years too. Hauppauge Digital skyrocketed 3,316 percent from $2.81 to $96. Avigen soared from $2.63 to $89 or +3,284 percent. Winners Internet shot 1,329 percent from $0.56 to $8. Aspect Telecommunications jumped from $6.38 to $70 or +997 percent.

At the end of the 90s Wall Street was pushing momentum buying. Based on technical analysis, investors bought stocks with soaring volume and prices at the 52-week high under the assumption that the momentum would push the price even higher. Foolish investors swallowed this flawed theory hook, line and sinker.

The media created a new "hero" called a day trader. The day trader made a living buying and selling stocks on the computer. In theory, the trader would take a few pennies profit on several thousand shares many times during the day and this would add up to a huge amount of profit. Everyone wanted to be a day trader.

It's ironic that the peak for individual investing, Internet investment chat rooms, momentum investing, day trading and the all-time market index highs occurred in the second week in March 2000. When the bubble burst, the majority of day traders and momentum investors were wiped out.

While a new investing "system" becomes the craze every few months, I've found the only system that consistently works during both good and bad markets. It's not flashy, and it doesn't have gimmicks. It's just finding the bargain – looking for a quality company with good fundamentals that is selling near its 52-week low price.

Smart investors have several characteristics in common. They have the courage to buy a stock when everyone else seems to be selling. They must have patience to hold when the stock doesn't move. The final characteristic is the wisdom to sell when they've made a nice profit. 'Buy Low, Sell High' is more than a catchy phrase, it's the only real way to continuously make money in the stock market.

Chapter

How and When to Sell
Your Stock

While the price you pay for your stock will directly affect how much profit you make, the other half of the transaction is the price at which you sell your investment. It's hard to wait for your stock to go down to a low price before you purchase it. It's even more difficult to decide when to take your profit.

I'm a big believer in determining an exit strategy before purchasing a stock. Basically your exit strategy is taking the time to figure out what you think the stock can do. You need to ask yourself the following questions.

- Is it a long or short-term investment?
- Do I think I can get a 25, 50, 100 percent return or more?
- Do I need that money in a specific time period? (i.e., to pay my child's college fees in 6 months?)

Because most investors don't think about the variables and possibilities, selling becomes more problematic. Low-priced stocks can be especially frustrating because they usually are very volatile, quickly shooting up and falling even faster. If you aren't ready to take advantage and hesitate, you can lose the opportunity to make a nice profit.

During the bull market of 1999 and in early 2000 we saw a tremendous number of stocks soar 200 to 500 percent. (A few outstanding ones skyrocketed even higher.) Some of our real CHEAP stocks had tremendous moves. Examples of these are: Emerson Radio (+1,700 percent), MicroTel (+1,100 percent), Nexell Therapeutics (+1,320 percent), Fonix (+1,220 percent), and Dauphin Technology (+2,738 percent). I remember speaking with one subscriber who bought 100,000 shares of Fonix (OTCBB – FONX) at $0.25. After several months the stock began to move, and by February 2000 it soared to a high of $3.30. That subscriber called a couple times when the stock was between $2.50 and $3.00. While I can't give individual investment advice, I suggested she think about taking some profits off the table. Unfortunately she heavily relied on investment chat lines and was convinced that the stock would go to $100. As I write this, Fonix is trading at $0.22 after executing a 1/40 reverse stock split. I don't know if she ever took any profit.

Fonix is a great example of why investors need to be realistic about dreams of one stock making them rich. It does happen, but most investors will never be lucky enough to parlay a $1,000 investment into $100,000. The investor who bought 100,000 shares of Fonix had a shot at some great profits, but was blinded by greed. Look at what she could have done.

Original purchase of 100,000 shares of Fonix @ $.25 for $25,000	
stock at $.50	$25,000 potential profit
stock at $1.00	$75,000 potential profit
stock at $1.50	$125,000 potential profit
stock at $2.00	$175,000 potential profit
stock at $2.50	$225,000 potential profit
stock at $3.00	$275,000 potential profit
stock at $3.30 high	$305,000 potential profit

What can we learn from this? *Never be afraid to take a profit.* Most investors look back to March 2000 and share the same desire. They wish that they had taken more profits.

While no one knows the lowest price a stock will hit before it begins to move upward, or the highest price it will achieve before starting to fall, the smart investor can use certain techniques to buy or sell a stock at the best price. This chapter lists some general guidelines for obtaining a good profit.

SELL OR AVERAGE DOWN?

"Cutting your losses" is a phrase that is commonly used by many Wall Street brokers, analysts and newsletter writers. They advise that if your stock price falls 10 to 20 percent, sell the stock to cut your losses. One well-known adviser recommends selling if your stock falls 8 percent.

I don't agree with this advice because many volatile stocks can easily drop more than that before soaring upward. If your stock price falls, you should review the company to learn whether there has been any negative news that caused the price to drop. Sometimes an investor will sell a large block of stock because he needs the money and that causes the price to tumble even though the company is still in excellent financial shape. If there doesn't seem to be a valid reason for the decline in the stock price and it has dropped 25 to 30 percent, you may be wiser to average down. (See page 125 for more information on averaging down.)

TAKING YOUR PROFIT, PROTECTING YOUR PROFIT

A common investment mistake is falling in love with your stock and never selling it. For example, the investor watches his stock price rise to the point where he has a good profit. However, he doesn't sell; instead, he watches the stock price fall back again. The investor has forgotten that the main reason for buying a company's stock is to *make a profit!*

It's all right to love your company, but look at it another way. If you love the company so much, wouldn't you want to own more of it? You can, if you are willing to sell when you have a profit, and buy it back after the price falls.

If you have $2,000 and like a stock that is selling at $1, you can buy 2,000 shares. If the stock goes up to $3 and you sell, you now have a profit of $4,000 plus your original $2,000. Keep following the stock as it falls back again to $1.25. After reanalyzing the company to make sure that it still is a good investment, you can purchase 4,800 shares with your $6,000. Let's say the company's stock continues on its upward cycle and hits $2.50. You sell the stock and now have $12,000, which gives you a $10,000 or +500 percent profit and allows you to purchase even more shares of stock when the price again falls near its low. You can love a stock, but don't let it blind you to making a profit.

Perhaps one of the most important things to remember when figuring your profit on an investment is to look at the price move in percentages rather than in dollars and cents. If you don't, you can easily get confused. For example, you have $3,500 to invest and buy $1,500 of stock A, which is selling at $2 per share, and $2,000 worth of stock B, which costs $40 a share. You would be able to buy 750 shares of stock A and 50 shares of stock B.

$1,500 ÷ $2 per share for stock A   = 750 shares
$2,000 ÷ $40 per share for stock B   = 50 shares

If stock A goes up $0.75 and stock B increases by $5, off hand it looks like stock B has performed better. However, if you actually figure the profit percent, you see a different story:

750 shares x $.75 increase   = $562.50 profit
$562.50 profit ÷ $1,500 purchase price   = 38%

50 shares x $5 increase   = $250 profit
$250 profit ÷ $2,000 purchase price   = 13%

This example illustrates why it is important to look at your profits in percentages.

After purchasing a stock, the wise investor will spend a little time along with his money and check the stock's price on the Internet or in the local newspaper (if the stock is listed). If the stock hardly moves, checking the price every week may be often enough. However, if the stock is more volatile, it is a good idea to look at its price at least once a day.

In December 2001, I recommended Cytogen (NASDAQ – CYTO) at $2.35. The stock almost doubled to $4.50 in three weeks and then fell back under $3 in two more weeks. If an investor didn't check Cytogen's stock price regularly, he would have missed the opportunity to make a very nice profit!

TIPS FOR WHEN TO PLACE A SELL ORDER

Lower priced stocks are more volatile than the blue chips and they can move 50 or even 100 percent very quickly. When you've made a nice paper profit, you should consider selling at least part of your investment. Certain telltale signs can indicate the possibility that a stock's price will fall. The smart investor looks for these signs and takes them into consideration.

The Company Announces a Reverse Stock Split

In my opinion, one of the worst decisions a company can make is to execute a reverse stock split. In most instances, I have seen that maneuver hurt instead of help the stock price. To understand a reverse stock split, you must first learn about a regular stock split.

A *stock split* occurs when a corporation's board of directors decides that the stock price is too high. The company can split the stock (and thus the price) to make it more attractive to institutional buyers and other investors.

Figure 12.1 Example of a 3-for-1 Stock Split

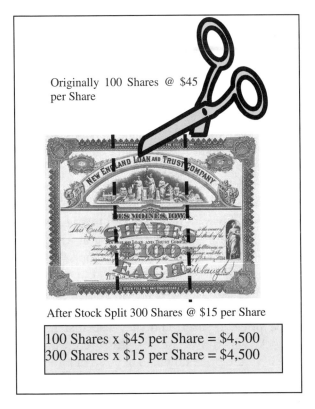

Originally 100 Shares @ $45 per Share

After Stock Split 300 Shares @ $15 per Share

100 Shares x $45 per Share = $4,500
300 Shares x $15 per Share = $4,500

Many stock-split configurations are possible: 1.5 for 1; 2 for 1; 3 for 2; 4 for 3; 5 for 1; and 5 for 2 are just a few examples. How does a stock split work? Figure 12.1 shows a 3-for-1 split. Before the stock split, 100 shares of stock were worth $45 per share. Once the stock is split, the 100 shares become 300 shares, each worth $15. If you multiply the shares by the price, you will see that the dollar value is the same, even though the number of shares is different. Why go through the bother of a stock split? Many companies split their stock to make the price more attractive to investors. The company's total number of outstanding shares also is increased by the stock split. If the company had 2 million shares outstanding before the 3-for-1 stock split, it would have 6 million shares outstanding after the split.

As you probably guessed from the name, a *reverse stock split* is just the opposite of a stock split, so instead of ending up with more shares at a lower price, the reverse stock split creates fewer shares at a higher price. For example, if a $.50 company has 45 million shares and decides to execute a 1-for-10 reverse split (see Figure 12.2), the company would end up with only 4.5 million shares at a price of $5 each. Likewise, an investor with 5,000 shares would have 500 shares after the reverse stock split.

Figure 12.2 Example of a 1 for 10 Reverse Stock Split

| | Company | | Investor | |
	Before	After	Before	After
Shares	45 million	4.5 million	5,000	500
Price	$.50	$5	$.50	$5
Value	$22.5 million	$22.5 million	$2,500	$2,500

In more than 20 years of recommending stocks, I have watched more than 100 companies execute reverse splits; and about 95 percent of them ended up lower in value than before the reverse split. My statistics indicate that in most cases, after a reverse stock split the shareholders' value decreases 35 to 50 percent or more.

Why does this happen? It's simple. One day the stock is selling at $0.50 per share, and the next day it is selling at $5. There is a resistance factor involved. When a stock's price suddenly shoots up without any substantial gain in profits to bolster the price, the market, which has valued the stock at $0.50, resists the higher price, causing it to fall.

In addition, many specialists and traders are aware that reverse stock splits cause the price to drop, and they use that to their advantage by shorting the stock, which also applies pressure on the price. Even small investors help drive the price down. They see that their stock has gone up in price (without realizing that they have proportionately fewer shares), and they sell for a profit (they think). A large amount of "profit taking" can send the stock price tumbling, causing even more selling.

It's ironic that one of the biggest proponents of reverse splits is the NASDAQ market. Because of the NASDAQ SmallCaps' and National Market System's $1 minimum selling price requirement, many companies find themselves in a no win situation. If their stock price remains under the $1 minimum for too long, they are given the choice of executing a reverse stock split or being delisted to the OTC Bulletin Board exchange. I've recommended that several companies choose to be delisted to the OTC Bulletin Board as the lesser of two evils. The primary reason I don't like reverse stock splits is that it's a "quick fix" and does nothing to improve the company's fundamentals.

On my January 2000 Hotline, I recommended a small biotech company, Nexell Therapeutics, Inc. (NASDAQ – NEXL) at $1.18. The stock soared to an all-time high of $16.75 (+1,319 percent) in three months. However, on June 15, 2000 Nexell made a major blunder when it announced a 1 for 4 reverse stock split with the price then at $4. After the 1 for 4 reverse the stock price was approximately $16. It plunged from that point eventually reaching an all-time low of $0.60 on November 20, 2001. That's a 96 percent loss!

I have a very simple philosophy about reverse stock splits. As soon as I hear that a stock in my portfolio is going to execute a reverse split, I sell. If I still like the company, I can probably buy more shares for a much lower price a few months after the split takes effect.

The Company Raises Cash Through an Equity Offering

A company that needs additional working capital often will raise the money through an equity offering. The company can offer a portion of its equity through issuing additional common stock, preferred stock, rights, warrants, private stock and convertible or junk bonds. However, with each offering, the additional shares eventually dilute the value of the company's existing shares. When a company completes such a financing, about 90 percent of the time its stock price falls. The larger the financing, the greater the dilution and, correspondingly, the farther the price will drop.

When a shareholder receives the quarterly report, he should check the amount of cash the company has. A drastic drop in the company's cash can signal trouble for the stock's price. If the company is in a cash-intensive industry such as the entertainment or high-technology fields, be very careful if the cash drops below $1,000,000.

To compare the company's cash position, you will need to refer to its annual or quarterly reports. In the report's consolidated balance sheet section, the assets will list cash and will show figures for two or more years. (Sometimes there will also be a cash equivalents column, which shows stocks or other investments. They should be considered as cash when determining the company's cash position.) In the following example the cash has radically decreased.

	2003	2002	2001	2000
Cash	$97,369	$4,680,274	$7,747,321	$10,346,837

These figures indicate that the company has been using about $3 to $4 million in cash each year for working capital. With only $97,369 in 2003, the company will probably need to supplement its cash. If the company is to survive, it will have to obtain more working capital from sales, a loan or an offering of more shares through its investment banker.

If the company chooses to offer more shares, it will dilute the value of the existing shares; this usually will cause the stock price to fall. When the smart investor foresees the need for an offering, he can sell the stock. Most of the time, the investor can repurchase shares after the additional shares have caused the stock price to fall.

Certain industries are not so cash-intensive, and the company may not need such large cash amounts. Pacer Technology (NASDAQ – PTCH) is a fine example of a company that usually averages under $100,000 cash on hand. However, this works for Pacer because the company has virtually no long-term debt and expansion is financed from its increasing sales.

Perhaps the best strategy when comparing the cash position in previous years is to look for a drastic decrease. Further research should show if the decrease was caused by an acquisition (which could be very positive for the company) or from other more negative sources. By following the company's cash position, the investor can decide if the company will need to find some method of raising working capital and whether the investor should consider selling his shares.

Large Increases in Inventory

While reading the balance sheet, check the inventory position, especially if the company manufactures products. Many times a huge increase in the company's inventory indicates the start of trouble. When inventory builds in the warehouse, besides the obvious fact that it isn't bringing in revenues, it also creates a drain on the company's finances by the expenses incurred from the additional inventory financing, warehousing, taxes and insurance. If the company's earnings have also dropped, this could mean serious problems on the horizon, so the investor should consider selling the stock.

The Company Merges with Another Company

When one company buys another, typically the stock price jumps in anticipation of the merger and then comes down to the agreed-on price on the day of the official consolidation. The interest created by the news brings in investors, which raises the price, but after the merger, the interest subsides and so does the stock price.

In addition, combining the two newly consolidated companies may temporarily cause substantial increases in expenses. Shuffling job responsibilities, early retirement costs, expenses for closing redundant facilities, etc., can cause a huge drain on profitability until the reorganization is complete and new personnel learn their jobs. Often the investor can sell the stock for a higher price just before the merger is completed and then buy it back at a lower price after the consolidation takes effect.

When a merger calls for the shareholders to receive one share of the new company for more than one share of the old, this is actually a disguised reverse stock split. For example, the shareholder must pay three shares of the old stock for one share of the new stock. If this happens to one of your stocks, sell it.

The Stock Price is Nearing a Resistance Level

A key factor in the *CHEAP Investor* philosophy is to sell a stock when everyone else wants it. In other words, when everyone else wants to buy the stock, its price will be high. That's the time to take your profit because you were wise enough to get into the stock when its price was low.

•   **Rule 10**   •

**Buy your stock when no one wants it and sell it
when everyone wants to buy.**

As buying interest increases, so does trading volume. The stock price moves upward until it hits a point that technical analysts call a *resistance level*. Basically it's a price ceiling at which selling starts to come into the stock. Resistance levels differ depending on a stock's price. Stocks trading for a few pennies can have resistance levels at every ten cents. Stocks trading between $1 and $10 usually experience resistance at the dollar level. For example a stock selling at $1.75 would have a resistance level at $2. If the price broke that barrier, then it's next resistance level would be $3. Stocks trading over $10 usually have resistance levels at $15 and $20. A stock selling at $20 or more would have resistance levels in $10 increments.

If a stock successfully hurdles one resistance level, then it will move toward the next resistance level. Most stocks need several attempts before they are able to break through a resistant level to move toward the next. A key indicator as to whether the stock will have the power to break through the resistance level is trading volume. If the volume falls as the price approaches the resistance level, the stock will probably not make it past that point. Once the trading volume falls, the stock price quickly follows as the chart below shows.

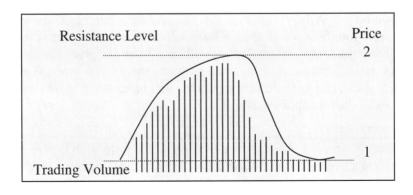

The goal is to sell your stock as the volume is going up. That's pretty hard to do unless you have a crystal ball. However by watching the trading volume, you can sometimes get an indication of whether the stock will continue past the resistance level or if it's losing steam.

MARKET SELL, LIMIT SELL, STOP LOSS AND STOP LIMIT ORDERS

You have invested time and effort to research several stocks to discover a quality company at a low price, and now your efforts have paid off. The stock has risen 200 percent and it is time to take your profit. You can call your broker to enter either a market sell order or a limit sell order.

Market Sell Order

The vast majority of all sell orders are *market sell orders*. This type of order offers your shares of stock at the best prevailing price (market price) as soon as possible after the order reaches the exchange floor. This is the quickest way to sell your stock. If the stock trades well (several hundred thousand shares daily), your order should be executed immediately. However, if your stock is thinly traded (10,000 to 20,000 shares daily), you may find that the market makers sell your stock at a price much lower than you thought you would get.

Limit Sell Order

I recommend that investors use a *limit sell order*. Very simply, a limit sell order specifies a price and a time period during which the shares will be offered at that price. The limit order is good only for a day unless the investor requests that it be offered for a longer time period such as a week, month or "until canceled".

The shares may or may not sell. It's solely dependent on whether anyone wishes to pay the specified price. A limit sell order may be canceled at any time and another limit sell order can be entered at a higher or lower price depending on the circumstances.

If you bought ABC company at $1 and find the price has risen to $2, you can call your broker and enter a limit sell order offering your shares at $2.25. If the stock goes up to $2.25 it will be sold at that price. However, if it does not go up to $2.25, the stock will not be sold. As circumstances change, you can call your broker, cancel the sell order at $2.25 and enter a new order at whatever price you want.

Stop Loss Order

Investors can use a *stop loss order* to protect a profit of 100 percent or more. Ideally, you call your broker and set a certain price at which the stock will automatically be sold if it falls that low. If used correctly, the stop loss order is a good tool to protect your profit.

For example, if the ABC Company stock has risen to $2.25, the investor can enter a stop loss order with his broker at $1.88. If the stock falls to $1.88, it should automatically be sold. If the ABC Company's stock price continues to move upward, the investor would also raise the price at which the stop loss is set.

There is a technique to using the stop loss order. Remember, this is set to protect your profits. You don't really want to sell the stock because you believe it will continue to move upward; however, if it does start to fall, you won't end up back where you started (or worse).

Most stocks don't move straight up or straight down. In its upward cycle a stock may rise $0.10, fall $0.15, jump $0.25 and fall $0.12. The stop loss order has to allow some room for normal downward movement of the stock before it begins to rise again. In many instances the even-dollar price ($2, $3, $4, etc.) becomes a base as the stock falls back that far and then starts upward. Therefore a stop loss order should never be entered at an even-dollar amount. That is why in the previous example the stop loss was set at $1.88 rather than at $2.

Figure 12.3 Setting a Stop Loss Price

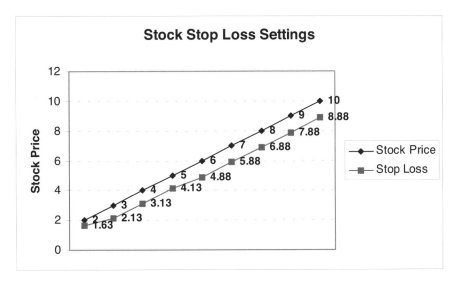

As you can see, it becomes a delicate balancing act to try to preserve as much profit as possible if the stock does plunge. However, you also don't want the stop loss price so close to the current stock price that the stock is sold, just because the price dipped down before rising again. If the stock is especially volatile, the stop loss may need to be set slightly lower. Once the ABC Company's stock rises to $2.75, the investor would raise the stop loss to $2.38. Avoid the $0.50 level, for the stock could easily fall that far. Figure 12.3 shows suggested guidelines for setting a stop loss price for a stock as it rises from $1.

Most discount brokers don't offer this service, but you still can make use of this technique by setting your own stop loss point and entering a sell order with your broker if the stock falls to that level. You will have to closely follow the stock price; however, it is worth the effort to avoid losing a good profit.

Stop loss orders work well with stocks trading large volume i.e., 750,000 shares or more daily. It does not work well with stocks trading much lower volume. I remember a friend who bought a stock at $2. It soared to $13 and was trading at $12.25 when he put a stop loss order at $11.70 for 5,000 shares. The market makers saw the order and sold 100 shares of his stock at $11.70 and the rest of his shares were sold at $10.70. Immediately after the market makers bought those shares at $10.70, they raised the stock price to $12.75. It was an expensive lesson to learn that you can't trust the market makers not to take advantage.

Stop Limit Order

Most investors confuse Stop Loss and Stop Limit Orders. Both are used to protect your profit or cut losses and are set at a price lower than the current market price. If the stock backs off to that price, then the broker will enter an order to sell the shares at the *market*. The example in the paragraph above illustrates the hazards of offering your stock at the market price.

I prefer to use a stop limit order, which is a combination of a stop loss and a limit order. It works the same as a stop loss order except that once it hits your stop price it becomes a limit order (specified price) rather than a market order (any price the market makers want to offer).

In the above example, if the investor would have set a stop limit order at $11.70 once the stock fell to that level, chances are he would have received that price for the stock. However, if the stock is falling fast, it may not get sold.

TAX SELLING AND THE JANUARY EFFECT

As the end of each year approaches, many brokers, accountants and financial planners recommend that their clients check their portfolios to determine whether they have any stocks that are in a paper-loss position. (The stock's current price is lower than the price at which the stock was purchased.) If so, the brokers advise their clients to sell the stock and take the loss for tax purposes.

I disagree with the timing of this strategy. Statistics show that most low-priced stocks are closer to their 52-week low price in November and

December (probably due to other investors selling for a tax loss and driving down the price). Because the investor can sell for a tax loss at any time during the year, he would be much wiser to sell at the point that he determines the investment has become unprofitable.

•   **Rule 11**   •

**Never sell a stock in December
just to take a tax loss.**

However, the investor shouldn't indiscriminately sell a stock for a tax loss without analyzing it first. Because low-priced stocks seem especially susceptible to the end-of-the-year falling price, and if the company is a good investment and the price has just dropped, the wise investor should buy more shares rather than sell for a loss.

One thing to consider when selling stock for a tax loss is that, if you are in the 28 percent tax bracket and you sell a stock in late December for a $1,000 loss, you save only $280 in tax dollars. If the stock was a bad investment, then $280 is better than nothing. However, if the stock is a quality company, it could easily rise higher than the $280 tax credit after the beginning of the year. For example, I recommended Crown Cork & Seal Inc. (NYSE – CCK) in December 2001, after the stock was hammered to $0.80. The stock soared in January 2002 to $4.90. Investors who held their shares or bought more at $0.80 saw their investment soar over 600 percent in about six weeks.

Tax selling causes the price of many stocks to drop. When other investors see the price of their stock falling, they panic and sell, causing the price to fall further and creating some excellent bargains. The individuals who sold for the tax loss now have money to invest. However, they wait until after the first of the year for tax purposes, which generates a corresponding upswing in price in January. This phenomenon, called the January Effect, normally results in low priced stocks far outpacing blue chip stocks.

Smart investors don't follow the crowd; instead, they are contrarians. This approach is just another way of saying, "buy low and sell high". Contrarians use the January Effect to their advantage and buy good-quality, lower-priced stock in December when the prices have dropped and sell in January or February for a good profit.

A stock's price is determined by supply and demand. That is, if more people want to buy a stock than there are shares available from people who want to sell, the stock price will rise. Likewise, if there are more sellers than buyers, the stock price will fall. If you invest contrary to the masses, you can buy your quality stock while there is little demand for it, and the price is low. Then when other investors become interested in the stock, and the price increases, you can sell it for a profit. Using this strategy to find the bargains, investors can make some great profits with the January Effect.

THE PARTIAL PROFIT STRATEGY

Near the end of 2001, I wrote an editorial about a smart subscriber who bought Argosy Gaming (NYSE – AGY) at $2.25 and CarMax (NYSE – KMX) at $1.56 after reading buy recommendations in my newsletter. This savvy investor sold 25 percent of each stock when they doubled, 25 percent when they tripled, 25 percent after they quadrupled and then hung on until he had the opportunity to sell the remaining 25 percent of Argosy at $28.25 and CarMax at $19.25. Needless to say, he was a very happy subscriber.

By taking some of his profits off the table, he could sit back and still smile even if the stock backed off to his original purchase price. Because he had confidence that Argosy and CarMax would move higher, he hung on to some of the stock. His strategy worked. As the stock moved higher, he was able to take greater profits.   If the stock had fallen back to where he bought it or below, he had capital from the profits he took to buy more shares. It was a win/win situation.

This strategy works well on stocks that have the potential to move even higher. Needless to say, if your stock has exhibited some of the triggers for selling mentioned previously in this chapter, you should consider taking all your profits.

Chapter

13

Profiting from Market Volatility

For the last decade, market volatility has intensified. The root of this increase lies in the stock market crash of 1987, which was the largest one-day plunge in the stock market. Ironically, most people aren't aware that the rebound the day after that crash was the second largest one-day move in the market.

In 1981, when I started writing *The CHEAP Investor*, the DOW was hovering around 750, and it was common to see a 15-point drop. With the DOW around 10,000 today, a 200-point fall is considered a major plunge. Both drops are only 2 percent of the market, but the average investor perceives the 200-point drop as scary. Perhaps the incessant news media play-by-play of the stock market has something to do with that. It's easy to be scared out of the market by a big-name analyst who solemnly predicts gloom and doom. You can't watch the news without hearing about something that's gone wrong with the stock market. Smart investors learn to ignore the panic peddlers and look for the bargains.

During the bull market of the 90s, the American public received a great education in Capitalism. They saw small high-tech companies become large successful companies, creating millions of jobs. Their success made billions of dollars for shareholders who were courageous enough to buy when the companies were still struggling.

Thirty years ago Kmart, General Motors and IBM were the pacesetters. Today a new generation of companies – Wal-Mart, Microsoft and Intel – have become industry leaders. As the success stories multiplied, the number of households investing in the market soared to over 60 percent.

At one time an investor could purchase a quality stock, put it in a safe-deposit box and forget about it, while it grew over the years into a nice nest egg for retirement. Today investing is more complex. Instead of putting away your stock and letting it grow, the playing rules have changed. The vast majority of low-priced stocks are cyclical, and smart investors usually can make more by purchasing a stock near its 52-week low and selling near its high than by holding it for long-term appreciation.

COMPUTERIZED PROGRAM TRADING

Times change. Several cable networks are devoted solely to the stock market during trading hours. The networks carry various stock-oriented programs that show the trades on the NYSE, Amex and NASDAQ at the bottom of the screen. This instant information has certainly made volatility much more of a factor in the movement of the market.

Computers have revolutionized the stock market. Information that was once available only to Wall Street professionals is now available to all. Orders to buy and sell stocks, bonds, mutual funds, etc. are transmitted around the world at the touch of a finger. Computers provide instant confirmation of trades, up-to-the-second quotes for stocks and diverse information that normally would not be easily accessible to the small investor. Not only is computerized information a tremendous asset for the investor, it is vital to institutions, large brokerage firms and portfolio managers.

Computerized program trading was spawned by high-speed communications and computerized stock trading. Because the trader can react so quickly to market changes, program trading is an invaluable tool that is used and abused.

For better or worse, it has totally changed the marketplace, causing tremendous market volatility in a short period of time. Program trading was a major culprit behind the stock market crash of 1987. While this crash happened many years ago, we can still learn from it.

VOLATILITY – A LEGACY OF THE CRASH OF 1987

The stock market crash of October 1987 was the first indication of how powerfully computerized trading could impact the market. That's why stock market historians still study the crash today. Stock market volatility became a major issue because of the crash, and restrictions on the amount of upward or downward swings have been put into place to avoid plunges such as the one we experienced then.

On October 19, 1987, the stock market, as measured by the Dow Jones Industrial Average, experienced the largest single-day movement in its history. Unfortunately, the movement was down – 508 points or about 22 percent. This disastrous plunge caused widespread investor panic. Stock market analysts and economic experts predicted a great depression or at least a major recession for 1988. It didn't happen.

Two days after the 508-point plunge, I wrote the following in an editorial for *The CHEAP Investor*:

> "We believe the blue chip stocks were at record high prices because of greed. Most were extremely overpriced, and then institutional buyers (who own a large percentage of blue chips) panicked and sold all day Monday (October 19), causing a 22 percent drop in the Dow.
>
> By Tuesday, those embarrassed institutional buyers realized that the blue chips were now at unrealistically low prices and began buying them back...There is no doubt that what happened the week of October 19, 1987, will be remembered for the rest of our lives. Since investments are measured over a long period of time in peaks and valleys, hopefully we can look back at this valley as a great investment opportunity."

It was mainly the higher-priced and blue chip stocks that suffered major losses on October 19. However, October 20 was more disastrous for the small investor. As the media whipped itself into a frenzy about the stock market crash, the small investor understandably became anxious and confused. The 20th saw an influx of sell orders from small investors in lower-priced stocks. In some cases, a vicious cycle was created as mass selling caused the stock price to decline further, causing more panic selling.

For several months after the crash, most of the "experts" were still predicting various forms of economic doom. I disagreed. The economic indicators were all positive, and while many investors had the breath knocked out of them, I didn't think the crash was going to have that drastic an effect on the economy. I wrote in the January 1988 editorial,

> "The October 19 panic taught us that 'investor followers' bought outrageously overpriced stocks because everyone said they would go up. The investor followers sold their stocks because everyone else was. Now investor followers are totally confused and buying nothing because no one else is.
>
> There is no doubt that October 19, 1987 will leave lasting scars on all of us and particularly the financial industry, but I have not seen any indication of any major effect on the rest of the economy."

Since it was an election year and interest rates and inflation were stable, I projected 1988 would be a good year for the market. Because stock prices had fallen so low, I thought the January Effect would be a big factor in 1988. Looking back at that year, the crash had little lasting effect on the market. It rebounded in 1988 and smart investors who grabbed the bargains profited from their foresight.

VOLATILITY CAUSED BY THE MIDDLE EAST OIL CRISIS

In 1990, investors had the opportunity to profit during the huge drop in the Dow Jones Industrials from 3,034 in June to 2,350 in October. The Iraqi invasion of Kuwait on August 2, 1990, caused oil prices to soar and inflamed the stock crisis. The invasion precipitated an almost 700-point drop, which occurred over a four-month period, as oil prices at the pump shot upward.

That 700-point drop was far more devastating than the 500-point drop in 1987 because it was a long-term decline, unlike the 1987 plunge which had a good recovery the next day. The combination of continually falling stock prices and rising gasoline prices crushed investor confidence and kept many from investing in potentially lucrative undervalued stocks. According to the Consumer Confidence Index, which hit a high of 82 percent in June, consumer confidence fell to a low of 68 percent by the end of 1990.

The panic resulting from the crisis caused many quality stock prices to plunge to the point where they were very undervalued. Investors who follow the contrarian philosophy realize that this is a great opportunity. It just takes courage to buy your bargain stock when everyone else is selling.

THE LAST DECADE IN THE MILLENIUM

Every day we hear some analyst or newscaster predict that this event or that will have a major effect on the stock market. The chart in Figure 13.1 shows the major events in the 1990s; and yet the DOW, with few exceptions, reacted with minor bumps as it continued to move ever upward.

The Gulf War in 1990 and Middle East oil crisis took the market down to a low of 2,350. Investors who came into the market at that low in October 1990 were happy to see it recover and then move steadily upward to hit a high of 4,000 in January 1994. The 4,000 barrier proved tough to break. One major stumbling block was the Clinton Administration's effort to nationalize healthcare. If passed, the rules would have impacted one-eighth of the U.S. economy. Wall Street and investors nervously got out of the market.

Figure 13.1 Volatility in the Century's Last Decade

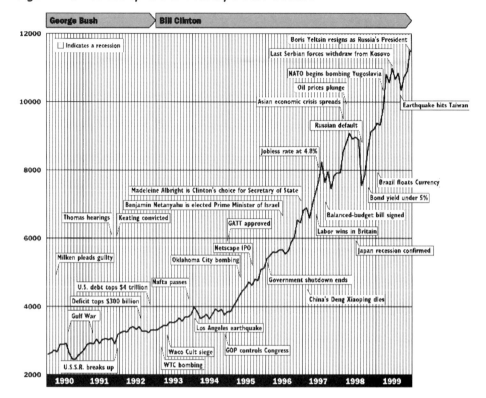

In November 1994, the power scale became balanced as voters gave the Republicans control of Congress. With a Republican Congress, Democratic president and the Contract with America calling for a balanced budget, tax limits and an amendment to restore fiscal responsibility to Congress, the economy started humming. By mid 1997, the market had shot up to 8,000.

The Balanced Budget bill was signed and the market again ran to hit a new high in 1998. The Russian Default hammered the market back to where it was before the Balanced Budget Bill was signed. About this time the bond market interest rates fell to under 5 percent, and institutions shifted to buying stocks. The market soared more than 2,500 points over the next eight months.

By the end of the decade Internet and high tech stocks fueled the market surge. Internet trading opened the door to more investors than ever before. Experienced investors and novices who wanted to get into the action invested huge sums into stocks. Climbing ever higher, the indexes hit all-time highs in the second week of March 2000.

That's when the bubble burst. Interest rates and oil prices started moving upward and the extremely overvalued Internet and high tech stocks started to plunge. Over the next three years almost $7 trillion of investor wealth was lost. The NASDAQ plummeted over 65 percent and the DOW fell almost 50 percent. An important lesson can be learned from this experience. Take at least some of your profits when you have them.

9/11 ATTACKS CREATE NEW VOLATILITY

The market has always had its ups and downs. However, one of the best examples of volatility is how the market reacted to the 9/11 terrorist attacks. After the attacks, panic selling by individual investors caused a dramatic market plunge.

In one week, the market experienced the largest drop in its history. During that time the Dow plunged 14 percent to 8,235 and the NASDAQ plummeted 16 percent to 1,423. Fearful individual investors cashed in over $30 billion of mutual funds in September. That number far exceeded the previous record of $20 billion. Ironically, panic selling by individual investors historically signals the bottom of the market. This proved to be the case once again.

Investors were devastated. The media had a field day painting a picture of imminent catastrophe. They gleefully reported the economy was ailing and ran daily stories of major layoffs. Wall Street analysts forecast a gloomy economy and market. It was probably the most difficult time since I started writing *The CHEAP Investor.*

I knew that my subscribers were looking to me for direction, so I spent the next 10 days analyzing the situation. The Hotline I recorded on September 21 would be crucial, and I decided to take a stand. My instinct and research were telling me that we were near the bottom. I told my Hotline subscribers to start positioning themselves for the next upward move. I wrote on the October 2001 issue,

"It's no wonder that investors were nervous when the stock market reopened. The media bombarded us with a bleak picture – the economy is ailing, there will be tens of thousands of layoffs, the bombing will have a devastating effect on the economy and the stock market. Who wouldn't be scared?

As much as the terrorists would like to take credit for ruining our way of life – it just isn't so. Yes, we have problems, but they were there before 9/11. The stock market has been trending downward for the past 18 months. The economy has been in a slump for over a year, and we're very close to meeting the statistical qualifications for a recession. Even tourist and business travel, especially hotel and airline reservations, have been declining for the past six months.

What the 9/11 tragedy accomplished is it focused attention on the economic downtrend and augmented it. Fear and uncertainty caused the record plunge in the stock market the week of September 17. That fear and uncertainty led to panic selling and record withdrawals from mutual funds.

Now for the good news. Those who study the market know that historically a sell-off by individual investors usually indicates that the market is near the bottom of its cycle. We think we've seen that sell-off and said so in our September 21 Hotline.

Generally the stock market turns around three to six months before the economy rebounds. The economy will be greatly stimulated by a huge amount of government spending on numerous programs including rebuilding, airline bailouts and new security measures. Those programs could infuse an additional $100 billion into the economy.

As lower interest rates take effect, we also look for increased business spending. The final piece in the recovery puzzle would be an economic stimulus plan that includes an increase in minimum wages and lower capital gains taxes. This should help the economy turn around in the first quarter of 2002."

The October 2001 issue contained several stocks that had been hammered to low prices, and they made some remarkable recoveries over the next few months.

Stock	Recommended Price	High Price	Percent Change
Autobytel (ABTL)	.70	3.35	378%
Sitel Corporation (SWW)	$.86	$2.50	191%
Crown Cork & Seal (CCK)	2.25	6.00	167%
Charles & Colvad Ltd. (CTHR)	1.00	2.63	163%
Variagenics Inc. (VGNX)	2.52	3.50	39%
MicroTel (MCTL)	.28	.44	57%

In retrospect I made the right choice to recommend getting back into the market. I'm not aware of any other analyst who called the bottom of the market and recommended to start purchasing shares. Over the next three months, the market rebounded with the NASDAQ bouncing back 40 percent and the DOW 22 percent.

PROFITING FROM COMMODITY PRICE VOLATILTY

While major market plunges can create many bargains, volatility in commodity prices can also affect stocks. For example, companies that mine gold, silver or precious gems usually see their stocks move upward or downward in response to increasing or decreasing prices for their particular commodity.

Several times in the early and mid 80s small mining stocks flew when their specific commodity (gold, silver, copper or platinum) soared. Investors, who bought when both the commodity prices and the individual stock's price were at extremely low levels, made huge profits. In the late 80s and throughout the 90s, gold and silver prices became stagnant. This was primarily due to better technology, which dramatically increased the amount of proven reserves. With a greater supply, the price of rare minerals fell. In addition, new technology allowed some companies to substitute more economical materials for gold and silver.

Oil stocks are another industry that responds well to commodity price volatility. Over a three-year period in the 90s I recommended four oil stocks when both their price and the price per barrel of oil were exceptionally low.

In April 1992, I issued a buy on Varco International Corporation (NYSE – VRC) at $4.88. Varco is a leading manufacturer of products used in the oil and gas industry. The stock soared to a high of $68 or +1,293 percent! In February 1993, I recommended Unit Corporation (NYSE – UNT) selling at $1.88. Unit engages in the production of oil and natural gas properties and the marketing of natural gas. The stock ran up 755 percent to a high of $16.

Dynamic Oil Corporation (NASDAQ – DYOLF) was recommended on the Hotline at $0.50. Dynamic is a small Canadian marketer and producer of natural gas. The stock quadrupled to $2. Perhaps the most interesting was Mitcham Industries (NASDAQ – MIND). I recommended it in the May 1995 issue at $2.75. Mitcham sells and leases seismic data acquisition equipment to the oil and gas industry. The stock soared to $33 or +1,100 percent!

Figure 13.2 Commodity Price Volatility

Stock	Recommended Price	High Price	Percent Change
Mitcham Industries (MIND)	$2.75	33.13	+1105%
Unit Corporation (UNT)	1.88	16.00	+865%
Varco International (VRC)	4.88	68.00	+1394%
Dynamic Oil (DYOLF)	.50	2.00	+300%

All four stocks hit their high price in the second week of October 1997, the same point that oil prices peaked. In the late 1990s and early 2000s, oil prices bounced up and down, but oil stocks did not respond as well as in 1997. Since then I have looked for the perfect combination of low oil and stock price, because I know this strategy will work again.

When volatility causes stock prices in a particular industry to fall, don't be so dazzled by the "bargains" that you forget to completely analyze the company. Make sure that it meets the normal requirements of price near the 52-week low, with good sales and increasing earnings.

VOLATILITY FROM THE WAR WITH IRAQ

One of the best examples of market volatility occurred in early 2003. Stocks were falling because of the fear of a war with Iraq. A nasty spiral developed, as the lower stocks fell, the more investors sold. In my March 2003 editorial, I warned investors "Don't Let Fears Scare You out of the Market." I wrote,

> "History is a great teacher, but if we don't learn from it, we are doomed to repeat our mistakes. That's certainly true of Wall Street's adverse reaction over the possibility of war with Iraq. This past month, war fears caused the DOW to lose much of the gains it had made since its October 2002 low point. Analysts are fanning the flames by predicting we will have higher oil prices, depressed consumer spending and weaker corporate profits. Individual investors, who have been bombarded with this depressing information, have quit buying stocks.

> Many investors are making a major mistake by letting the fear of a short-term event color their long-term decision process. When all is said and done, the war with Iraq (if it happens) will make little difference a year from now. In fact, we'll look back at this time and wish we had invested more money when the stock prices were so low."

It's ironic that once we went to war in Iraq, the market started to soar. Between March and the first week in June 2003, we saw the best bull market in small stocks in three years. For such a welcome change, I wrote in my July editorial,

> "As we review our recommendations since November, we're delighted at how well they have performed. They prove that our buy low, sell high philosophy is more than a catchy slogan – it works! Buying quality stocks at low prices can be extremely profitable, while momentum buying at new highs can be hazardous to your wealth."

In the eight-month period between November 2002 and July 2003, eighteen of my stock recommendations at least doubled. In some cases the stocks skyrocketed to three, four and even five times the original price, as shown in Figure 13.3.

Figure 13.3 Stock Recommendations that More than Doubled

Company	Buy Price	High Price	% Change
Secure Computing (SCUR)	3.66	9.25	+153%
Optika (OPTK)	.80	1.70	+113%
Wyndham (WBR)	.28	.77	+175%
Jacuzzi Brands Inc. (JJZ)	2.61	5.40	+107%
DUSA Pharm. (DUSA)	1.54	3.28	+113%
Advanced Powertech (APTI)	2.53	7.75	+206%
Audio Codes (AUDC)	2.10	5.80	+176%
Value Click (VCLK)	2.65	6.54	+147%
Alpha ProTech (APT)	.84	3.20	+281%
Catalyst Semi. (CATS)	2.20	5.80	+164%
Diacrin (DCRN)	1.05	4.65	+343%
Paradigm Genetics (PDGM)	.31	1.94	+526%
Barnes & Noble (BNBN)	1.10	2.68	+144%
Medarex, Inc. (MEDX)	2.80	7.35	+163%
Eagle Supply Group (EEGL)	.71	1.87	+163%
*Hauppauge Digital (HAUP)	1.18	3.95	+235%
*Internet Cap (ICGE)	.36	.96	+167%
*Mobility (MOBE)	.79	4.05	+413%

*Stocks recommended on the Hotline.

Late 2002 and early 2003 was a great time, as there were many quality stocks at bargain-basement prices. Investors who had the foresight to buy those stocks were rewarded with huge profits.

VOLATILITY IS HERE TO STAY

If you want to be a successful investor, instead of following the herd, be a contrarian. Perhaps one of the hardest lessons to learn is that when stock prices plunge due to volatility in an industry, or the stock market as a whole, this creates some fantastic bargains. A certain amount of courage is needed to think positively when almost everyone else is crying the blues. However, this approach can pay big dividends.

As long as you invest in a high quality company, even if the market plunges, the company will survive. At some point your bargain stock's price will move up from its undervalued position. You'll be smiling all the way to the bank, and your friends will wish that they had been farsighted enough to purchase so-and-so stock when it was cheap. The smart investor looks at volatility as an opportunity to profit.

Chapter

$$\boxed{14}$$

Investigate Before You Invest

I have a friend who is perhaps the most thrifty person I've ever known. When he buys a new car, he spends countless hours visiting various car dealers trying to get the best deal possible. Last time he spent six months and saved about $500 compared to the first deal he was offered. His favorite expression is "Salesmen hate to see me." He does this with every personal purchase, whether it's a computer, television or house. (He's been looking for a house for over eight years!)

Ironically, there's one area where he doesn't thoroughly investigate the deal – that's investing. When his broker calls, he usually gets talked into buying a "great little stock". Later, he will call me to ask what I think of the company. In many cases, I don't think much of his impulse purchases.

The other day he called and inquired about a stock. I quickly checked it out and said that, at $20 it was too high; but I'd be interested at $15. He admitted that he bought at $30 because his broker claimed to have a hot tip from a reliable source. His good intentions to seek the best deal fly out the window when he hears, "this investment will make you rich."

Learn from my friend. Research your investments just like you would any major purchase. This is one of the most important rules to successful investing.

Unwary investors get talked into great sounding investments and lose over $20 billion annually. High pressure con artists will gladly take your hard-earned cash for investments in private placements (investment in a company before it goes public), gold, oil wells, commodities, futures, options and let's not forget penny stocks.

```
•          Rule 12          •
Don't take anyone else's word.  Investigate
            before you invest!
```

A couple years ago, Enron Corporation magnificently imploded, leaving investors poorer, but wiser. Nothing's guaranteed. Enron was the fifth largest Fortune 500 company, and a Wall Street darling before it collapsed into bankruptcy due to fraud and accounting irregularities. Its accounting firm, Arthur Anderson, was considered one of the elite auditors. Now Arthur Anderson is struggling to survive. Investment fraud can happen anywhere, any time.

Whether your investment is listed on the NYSE or the OTC Bulletin Board, you need to check it out. The cheaper the stock price, the more you should research. A few years ago, an enlightening film "Boiler Room" showed how a brokerage firm can manipulate the stock of a small company. In the movie, the firm's owner had his brokers call people at random and hype the stock to the unsuspecting. His sole intention was to move the stock price high enough, so insiders could sell for a nice profit, before the whole house of cards fell down. One broker decided to visit the company only to find the building boarded up. The movie is an eye opener for those who assume that their broker must know what he is talking about. It certainly brought back memories of some of the more unscrupulous penny stock brokerage firms of the 1980s.

INVESTIGATE BEFORE INVESTING

Many times an investor becomes so bedazzled by how much money he can make that he forgets to ask any questions about the investment. Letting someone else make your investment decisions for you is certainly easier than taking the responsibility yourself; however, this makes you more susceptible to high-pressure investment scam artists.

Let's look at some investment scams. Of course, one ingredient that is always there is the investor's greed – a greed so great that it blinds the investor to the scam.

Classic Commodity Half-and-Half Scam

This scam has been used by aggressive brokers, who pick any volatile commodity, such as September pork bellies. Starting with a list of perhaps

500 prospective investors, the broker will call half of the investors and tell them to buy. The other half will be told to sell. Needless to say, 250 investors will be impressed with the broker's advice, because the pork bellies will either have moved up or down as predicted. Then the broker contacts the 250 people who were correctly advised and again divides the group in half, advising 125 to buy and 125 to sell another volatile commodity. Once that commodity either goes up or down, the broker contacts the group that has been twice correctly advised.

By now, that group of potential investors is extremely impressed with this financial wizard, and many will blindly follow his "superior" investment advice. This tactic provides the commodity broker with a steady stream of customers and commissions. Con artists have adapted this scam to futures, options and stocks.

How do you protect yourself from such a scam? One way is to investigate the broker before you trust him with thousands of your dollars. You can contact your state securities regulator, to see if they have more information about the company and the people behind it at http://www.nasaa.org/nasaa/abtnasaa/find_regulator.asp. The National Association of Securities Dealers can give you a partial disciplinary history on the broker or firm that's promoting the stock. If the broker or firm has used underhanded methods to sell securities previously, there's a chance that complaints have been lodged against him. You can contact the following associations:

U.S. Brokers and Brokerage Firms

National Association of Securities Dealers (NASD)
NASD Regulation
1735 K Street, NW
Washington, DC 20006
(301) 590-6500
Internet address: www.nasd.com

Commodity Brokers, Futures Brokers and Brokerage Firms

National Futures Association
200 West Madison Street, Suite 1600
Chicago, IL 60606
(800) 621-3570
Internet address: www.nfa.futures.org

SPOTTING AN INVESTMENT SCAM

Perhaps the best-known and most successful swindler of the twentieth century was Charles A. Ponzi, who emigrated from Rome to the United States in 1903. He has the dubious distinction of being the father of the "get rich quick" scheme. In 1919, Ponzi formed the Securities and Exchange Company in Boston.

Ponzi's scam was simple – lend me your money for 45 days, and I will pay back not only your principal, but 50 percent interest. The gullible public flooded him with money – almost $10 million. He paid the early investors with new investors' money. This strategy worked until July 1920, when Ponzi was bringing in more than $400,000 a day but couldn't repay earlier investors. Ponzi, the ultimate smooth talker, claimed, "The promise of a profit is not larceny, it is merely a promise, and a promise may or may not be kept according to the circumstances."

More than 80 years after Charles Ponzi's company was shut down, the Ponzi Scheme continues to flourish. Today's copycats create an aura of wealth with swanky offices, fine clothes and expensive cars (perhaps even a plane or helicopter). Potential investors are fed hints and suggestions about a "very profitable venture that is distributing extremely large profits to investors". Gullible and greedy investors still line up today to throw their money into such schemes.

Penny-Stock Scams

Scams have been rife in penny stocks, especially the OTC Bulletin Board and pink-sheet stocks. While a few investors get in on the ground floor of a legitimate company and sell the stock for a nice profit, most investors are not that fortunate. Penny stocks are risky investments. A typical penny stock is poorly financed with an uncertain future. Because of its low price and relatively small number of shareholders, its underwriter or market maker can easily manipulate the stock price.

One of the most well known examples is First Jersey Securities. In the brokerage firm's commercials, the chairman would step down from his helicopter and invite investors to "come grow with us". He would then promote the great investment opportunities in penny stocks. (You may have seen this ad several years ago when it ran during a Super Bowl game.) After years of run-ins with the SEC on the quality of the penny stocks that the brokerage firm sold, it was forced to close, leaving thousands of investors out in the cold.

Pump and Dump Schemes

One of the oldest scams is the pump and dump. Unscrupulous brokerage firms or inside investors promote a stock, in which they usually own hundreds of thousands of shares. As they convince investors to buy shares, they sell their own shares for a huge profit.

Variations of this scheme have exploded on the Internet. You might receive a newsletter purporting to have an excellent track record that will give you a free subscription. Aren't they sweet giving you a subscription out of the goodness of their hearts? Of course not!

Once they know you're gullible enough to subscribe, they send a multi-page report on a great little stock with a glowing recommendation about its potential to skyrocket. It's selling for only $0.85 per share, so what are you waiting for? They don't bother to disclose that they bought shares at $0.15 to $0.25, and they'll be selling at $0.85, while you're buying. Before the SEC shut them down, a 22-year old law student and his friends made over $350,000 in less than two months using this scam.

At least once a day I get a call from someone with a hot tip about a stock that's going to soar. A couple days ago, it was a stock trading at $1.50, but the caller swore that it would hit $10 by year-end. The first thing I did was to check the price chart to see where the stock had been trading. In that case, it had been at $0.25 just six weeks earlier. Why didn't they call me then? At $1.50 I said, "Thanks, but no thanks".

Internet Investment Scams

The Internet has revolutionized investing. It serves as an excellent resource for individual investors allowing them to quickly and easily research investment opportunities. Unfortunately, it is also an excellent tool for hucksters and crooks to take the hard earned money of naive investors.

Companies and individuals have access to a wide audience through the Internet. With a small investment of time, energy and money, promoters can reach millions of people with a Website. They can also send mass e-mails, post a note on an Internet bulletin board or join a live chat room.

In the past, most financial newsletters provided an unbiased opinion of the investment potential of various stocks. Since the newsletters' income source was subscription fees, their first allegiance was to their subscribers. The writers and editors put their reputation on the line each time they recommended a stock. If they made too many mistakes, the subscribers would go elsewhere and the newsletter would fold.

That changed with the advent of the Internet. While legitimate online newsletters can help investors gather valuable information, some online newsletters are tools for fraud. Instead of readers subscribing to the newsletters, companies compensate the newsletter writers with cash or securities to promote their stocks. Internet newsletters have proliferated over the past few years, and many just appear in your e-mail inbox. While it's not illegal, the newsletters are required by law to disclose any type of payment, how much they have been paid and who paid them. Unfortunately, some newsletters ignore this regulation. Instead they present themselves as a source of impartial information, while they actually stand to profit by convincing investors to buy or sell a particular stock.   They offer investors seemingly unbiased information, free of charge, about featured companies, or they recommend "stock picks of the month".

Sometimes these promoters are disguised as an independent research report on a specific company. I recently received a report touting a small technology company that was "positioned to dominate its industry". The price was $0.25 and, according to the report, its short-term target price was $3. I could already see my $2,500 investment to buy 10,000 shares soaring to $30,000.

I'm sure the allure of that huge profit caused a lot of investors to buy. Being more cynical, I checked the disclosure, which was in very small print at the end of the newsletter. I discovered that a third party gave the newsletter's parent company $48,000 in cash to represent the company for a year. In addition, it was given 200,000 shares of stock. Knowing that the newsletter has been "paid" for its opinion makes me very wary of their "unbiased" buy recommendation. Today that stock is trading at $0.01!

Chat Line Schemes

Internet bulletin boards and Chat lines have become very popular forums for investors to share information.   Typically, they feature "threads" made up of numerous messages on a particular investment opportunity.   While some messages may be true, many turn out to be fraudulent. Posters often pump up a company or pretend to reveal "inside" information about upcoming announcements, new products or lucrative contracts.

The major problem with these forums is, you never know who you're dealing with, or whether they are credible.   With the anonymity of an assumed Internet ID, a scam artist can hype or "flame" a company's stock depending on his ulterior motives.

People claiming to be unbiased observers who've carefully researched the company, may actually be company insiders, large shareholders or paid promoters. Because many bulletin boards allow users to hide their identity with multiple aliases, a single person can easily create the illusion of widespread interest in a small, thinly-traded stock by posting a series of messages under various names.   Wise investors should view such messages with a skeptical eye and always research the company before buying.

SCAMPROOFING YOUR INVESTMENTS

Following are eleven tips that investors should follow when considering an investment. Because purchasing stock may involve a lot of money, it can be an expensive lesson, if you make a mistake. While the vast majority of brokers and financial analysts are honest, you should be aware that there are unethical salespeople. Misrepresentation of a stock's value and outright fraud do occur.

1. Never buy any investment offered over the telephone or Internet without investigating. Always ask for written information about the investment so you can review it.

2. Beware of a broker or promoter who applies high pressure for you to buy immediately.

3. Check the references of any broker or promoter you don't know who tries to sell an investment to you.

4. Be suspicious of "guarantees" for quick or huge profits.

5. Never buy on tips or rumors. Get all the facts first. Many rumors of big contracts or revolutionary technologies never come to fruition. It is illegal to buy or sell stock based on "inside information", so be wary of supposedly confidential information.

6. Recognize that, in any investment program, past success does not guarantee success in the future.

7. If you don't understand something in a prospectus or a sales brochure, get advice.

8. Don't speculate unnecessarily. Speculation may be a worthwhile investment tool for knowledgeable, experienced investors who understand the risks involved. It is too risky for the average investor.

9. Be extremely careful with any investment that claims a much higher return than average. If a broker claims that he can guarantee you a certain percent profit, beware. There are no guarantees when investing in stocks.

10. Purchase stocks listed on the NYSE, Amex, NASDAQ or OTC Bulletin Board. Do not buy OTC pink-sheet stocks. Never buy an investment from a brokerage firm located outside the U.S. Don't buy if the investment is based outside the U.S. or only listed on a foreign exchange because they are subject to less stringent regulations. This is especially true for Canadian-based companies and U.S. companies that are only listed on Canadian exchanges. Unfortunately this group of stocks has had a large number of scams.

11. Listen to your intuition. After totally analyzing a potential investment, if you have any qualms about the stock, don't invest.

Weeding Out the Scams

I learned a long time ago that, determining which investments to avoid, is a major step in deciding what to buy. Whenever you receive an unsolicited telephone call or e-mail offering to help you make money by investing in a great little company, beware. By asking the following two questions, you can weed out many potential scams:

- *Where is the stock traded?* If the salesperson says, "the OTC market", ask where specifically. If it's either the pink sheets or a foreign exchange, avoid the stock.

- *How did the company go public?* Most companies go public through an Initial Public Offering of its stock by an underwriter. If the company was a shell, a blind pool or a self-underwriting, stay away from the stock. They usually have something to hide.

If you are interested in the stock, analyze the company's annual, 10-K and 10-Q reports. You can obtain that information on the Internet or by contacting the company. Don't let the salesperson rush you into investing before you receive this vital information. If the investment is a good one, it will still be there in the two or three days it might take you to research the company and make an educated decision.

REGULATION IN THE MARKET-THE SEC

Under the federal securities laws, the major responsibility for regulating the conduct of the individuals and companies that buy and sell securities, lies with self-regulatory organizations that are governed by the SEC. The SEC's primary objectives are to ensure that the securities markets operate in a fair and orderly manner, to assure that the professionals in the securities industry deal honestly with their customers and to guarantee that corporations make public all the pertinent information an investor needs to make an intelligent investment decision. The SEC serves as a watchdog to protect against fraud in the sale of securities, illegal sales practices, market manipulation and other violations of investors' trust by brokers and brokerage firms. The SEC can deny registration to securities firms, and in some cases, may impose sanctions against a firm or individual who violates federal securities laws. Abuses include misappropriation of customer funds or securities, and manipulation of the market price of a stock.

Self-regulatory organizations, such as the NASD (National Association of Securities Dealers), introduce rules to supervise trading and other activities, establish qualifications for professionals in the securities industry, control the behavior of their members, and discipline those members who ignore or break its rules.

Despite the protection provided by federal and state securities laws, it is essential that investors know that they have the final responsibility for their own protection. In particular, the SEC can't guarantee the worth of any security. Each investor must make that judgment for himself.

It is a good idea to check the SEC's library to see if any of the individuals connected with an investment have had sanctions imposed against them. SEC offices are located across the United States.

Securities Regulators:

U.S. Securities and Exchange Commission
450 5th Street, NW
Washington, DC 20549
(800) SEC-0330
Internet addres: www.sec.gov

North American Securities Administrators Assn, Inc.
Suite 710
10 G Street, NE
Washington, DC 20002
(202) 737-0900
Internet address: www.nasaa.org

Each state has its own securities regulator. You can find your regulator at the Website of the North American Securities Administrators Association.

According to the SEC's Website, here's a sampling of recent cases in which the SEC took action to fight Internet fraud:

"Francis A. Tribble and Sloane Fitzgerald, Inc. sent more than six million unsolicited e-mails, built bogus Websites, and distributed an online newsletter over a ten-month period to promote two small, thinly traded "micro-cap" companies. Because they failed to tell investors that the companies they were touting had agreed to pay them in cash and securities, the SEC sued both Tribble and Sloane to stop them from violating the law again and imposed a $15,000 penalty on Tribble. Their massive spamming campaign triggered the largest number of complaints to the SEC's online Enforcement Complaint Center.

Charles O. Huttoe and twelve other defendants secretly distributed to friends and family nearly 42 million shares of Systems of Excellence Inc., known by its ticker symbol "SEXI." Huttoe drove up the price of SEXI shares through false press releases claiming non-existent multi-million dollar sales, an acquisition that had not occurred, and revenue projections that had no basis in reality. He also bribed co-defendant, SGA Goldstar, to tout SEXI to subscribers of SGA Goldstar's online "Whisper Stocks" newsletter. The SEC obtained court orders freezing Huttoe's assets and those of various others who participated in the scheme or who received fraud proceeds. Six people, including Huttoe and Theodore R. Melcher, Jr., the author of the online newsletter, were also convicted of criminal violations. Both Huttoe and Melcher were sentenced to federal prison. The SEC has thus far recovered approximately $11 million in illegal profits from the various defendants.

Matthew Bowin recruited investors for his company, Interactive Products and Services, in a direct public offering done entirely over the Internet. He raised $190,000 from 150 investors. But instead of using the money to build the company, Bowin pocketed the proceeds and bought groceries and stereo equipment. The SEC sued Bowin in a civil case, and the Santa Cruz, CA District Attorney's Office prosecuted him criminally. He was convicted of 54 felony counts and sentenced to 10 years in jail."

The vast majority of all investment scams have one similarity – high-pressure sales tactics. If you are offered a deal that's just too good to be true, it probably is. The best way to handle high-pressure, incredible sales offers is just say no!

Chapter

$$\boxed{15}$$

Investing Without Using Money

Just like diets, there are numerous theories on how to make money in the stock market. Philosophies vary from momentum investing (buy high on the assumption that it will move higher) to CHEAP investing (buy quality, low-priced stocks). There's always a new strategy for investors to try. Unfortunately, most don't work as well as claimed.

In addition, investors are so excited by the new philosophy that they don't take the time to fully learn and apply that strategy. It's extremely important to check to see if the strategy will work for you BEFORE you invest your hard-earned money.

A painless way to test your expertise in buying and selling stocks is to simulate trading without actually investing the money. Simulation allows you to gain experience in trading stocks. It provides the opportunity to learn from your mistakes without risk.

SIMULATING A STOCK TRADE

Each time you purchase a stock you will receive a confirmation from your brokerage firm that details the stock transaction. The confirmation will look similar to the one in Figure 15.1.

Figure 15.1 Stock Confirmation

In accordance with your instructions, the transaction below is confirmed for your account and is subject to terms listed on the reverse side. Please refer to your account number when placing orders or making inquiries. Refer to the reverse side for instructions on endorsing and mailing certificates.

You Bought	You Sold	Security	Stock Symbol	Price	Trade Date
7,500		Creative Host Service	(CHST)	$1.16	3-25-02

Account Number	Gross Amount	Interest	Commission	Other	Net Amount
123456	$8,700.00		$19.95		$8,719.95

Frank Thomas
1000 N. Michigan Ave.
Chicago, IL 60606
Confirmation – Customer's copy. Retain for tax purposes

The stock confirmation has the following ten areas of interest:

1. You bought/you sold tells how many shares were purchased if the amount is in the "you bought" area or sold if in the "you sold" area.

2. Security gives the name of the stock you traded.

3. Stock Symbol gives the stock's symbol, which you can use to follow the price on Internet quote Websites.

4. Price is the cost per share for the stock.

5. Trade date shows the date the stock was bought or sold.

6. Account number is the number of your account with that brokerage firm.

7. Gross amount is the price per share multiplied by the number of shares.

8. Commission shows the fee charged by the brokerage firm to either buy or sell the stock.

9. Net amount is the total amount owed to the brokerage firm if you bought, or owed to you if you sold.

10. Name and address lists your name and address and should be checked for accuracy.

The stock confirmation indicates that on March 25, 2002, you bought 7,500 shares of Creative Host Services at $1.16 per share. The gross price is $8,700 plus $19.95 commission. Therefore you owe the brokerage firm a total of $8,719.95.

Stock Record Worksheet

When you simulate a stock buy, you want to include most of this information on your stock record. The blank form on page 170 provides space for all the vital information for a particular stock investment on one easy-to-read page. The first section includes pertinent information on the company. If you were simulating the purchase of Creative Host Services, you would complete it as shown in Figure 15.2.

Figure 15.2 Company Information

> **Stock Record**
> Company Name: Creative Host Services
> Address: 16955 Via Del Campo, Suite 110
> City:-San Diego   State: CA   Zip: 92127
> Telephone Number: (858) 675-7711
> Stock Exchange: NASDAQ   Stock Symbol: CHST
> 52-WeekHigh: $2.00   52-Week Low: $0.85

The "buy transaction" section contains all the important details of the stock purchase. At the bottom of the section you should write your reasons for buying the stock and the price you think the stock will hit. It would look like Figure 15.3.

Figure 15.3 Buy Transaction

> Date: 3/25/02   Stock Price: $8,700.00
> Number of Shares: 7,500   Plus Commission: $19.95
> Price per Share: $1.16   Purchase Price: $8,719.95
> Why you purchased the stock: Company is in good growth industry as travelers are spending more time in airports. Nine month financials show increasing revenues and earnings. Healthy balance sheet has book value of $2 per share. Company recently raised $5 million from private investors
> Profit Potential: 50-100% over the next year

When you decide that it is time to sell your stock, you would complete the two bottom sections. The "sell transaction" records the money you receive when you sold the stock. You also want to explain your reason for selling the stock, at that point. If you decided to sell Creative Host Services at $1.94, you would complete this section as shown in Figure 15.4.

The final section helps you to ascertain how well your investment worked for you. Complete the left-hand column first to determine your profit or loss. Then complete the right-hand column to calculate your percentage of profit or loss. Perhaps the most important part of the simulation is to analyze what you did right and what you did wrong in choosing your stock.

Figure 15.4 Sell Transaction

Date: __4/18/02__   Stock Price: **$14,550.00**
Number of Shares: __7,500__   Minus Commission: __$19.95__
Price per Share: __$1.94__   Amount Received: **$14,530.05**
Why you sold the stock: __Stock moved up 67% to near its 52-week high price of $2. I think the $2 level will prove to be a major resistance point so I'm taking my profit.__

The whole idea is to learn from the simulated transactions to avoid losing your money. Figure 15.5 shows how to complete the "profit or loss percentage" section for Creative Host Services. Writing all the details about your particular investment is a great educational experience. It also makes it easier to review your buy and sell transaction and learn from them.

Figure 15.5 Profit or Loss Percentage

Amount Received: __$14,530.05__
Purchase Price: __8,719.95__
Profit or Loss: __+5,810.10__
Divide Profit or Loss by Purchase Price to get the Percent
(5,810.10 profit ÷ $8,719.95 purchase price = .666 or 67%)
Percent Profit or Loss: __+67%__
What you learned from this transaction: __I have a 67% profit in less than four weeks. I think that the $2 level might be hard to break, so I'm taking my profit!__

Stock Price Data Sheet

The downfall of many investors is not following the stock after purchasing it. They spend the time to determine their best investment, but then get lazy or too busy to follow them. Consequently, they miss some great profit opportunities.

```
┌─────────────────────────────────────────────────────┐
│  •        Rule 13      •                              │
│  Follow your stock price so you don't miss major      │
│            profit opportunities.                      │
└─────────────────────────────────────────────────────┘
```

The stock price data worksheet (see the blank worksheet provided on page 171) makes it easy to follow your investments. You can record the stock price every day (which I recommend) or every week, depending on how volatile the stock is. The top section includes a little background information on the stock, including the 52-week high and low and the price you paid for the stock. These three figures are important in determining when you should sell your stock.

The main body of the worksheet allows you to enter the daily (or weekly) closing price and the amount it is either up or down. At the end of the week (or month), fill in the difference for that time period. Keeping this record will show how the stock trades are doing and will allow you to easily decide if you should sell the stock.

The stock price data sheet shown in Figure 15.6 illustrates how the daily price move on Creative Host Services might have looked. On the 18th day the stock hit a high of $2.08 and then started to fall. I entered a sell order at $1.94 and sold at that price.

ANALYZING THE TRANSACTION

When I originally researched Creative Host, I found that the company had good increasing revenues and earnings and the $1.16 price was very attractive. My objective was to sell the stock when it rose 50 percent, which I hoped to see over the next year. I didn't have to wait long. The stock shot up in just a matter of days and since I had achieved more than the 50 percent profit target, I decided to sell and take my profit. Creative Host turned out to be an excellent investment and my decision to sell was a wise one.

Taking the learning opportunity a step further, I reanalyze my stock transactions after six months and one year. This gives me the opportunity to reassess my decision to sell. Would I have been smarter to hold on?

Figure 15.6 Stock Price Data Sheet on Creative Host Services

Stock Price Data

52 Week High	Low	Company Name	Date Purchased	Price Per Share
$2.00	$0.85	Creative Host Services	3/25/2002	$1.16

Day or Week	Price per Share	Up or Down	Day or Week	Price Per Share	Up or Down
1	1.20	0.04	21		
2	1.23	0.07	22		
3	1.28	0.12	23		
4	1.29	0.13	24		
5	1.29	0.13	25		
Percent Change		11%	Percent Change		
6	1.40	0.24	26		
7	1.41	0.25	27		
8	1.40	0.24	28		
9	1.31	0.15	29		
10	1.21	0.05	30		
Percent Change		4%	Percent Change		
11	1.39	0.23	31		
12	1.40	0.24	32		
13	1.39	0.23	33		
14	1.40	0.24	34		
15	1.60	0.44	35		
Percent Change		38%	Percent Change		
16	1.60	0.44	36		
17	1.72	0.56	37		
18	1.94	0.67	38		
19			39		
20			40		
Percent Change		67%	Percent Change		

Selling Price: $1.94

If the stock continued to move up to say $9, then holding at least some of the stock might have been a wiser choice. Should I have just sold part of my shares? These questions have easy answers in hindsight. The answers aren't so straightforward when you don't have a crystal ball to see what the stock will do over the next few months.

I've learned my best strategy is to take a look at the stock's fundamentals when I'm considering selling. Do the fundamentals suggest that the stock is still undervalued? Do they indicate that the stock's price is unacceptably high, considering how poorly the company is doing? The answers to these questions can guide you in your decision to sell all or just a part of your shares.

Take the time to trade at least three to five stocks on paper before investing for real. The mistakes you make and the lessons you learn can help you become a wiser investor, without doing damage to your wallet!

<u>Stock Record Worksheet</u>

Company Name: _____

Address: _____

City:-_____ State: _____ Zip: _____

Telephone Number: _____

Stock Exchange: _____ Stock Symbol: _____

52-WeekHigh: _____ 52-Week Low: _____

Buy Transaction

Date: _____ Stock Price: _____

Number of Shares: _____ Plus Commission: _____

Price per Share: _____ Purchase Price: _____

Why you purchased the stock: _____

_____

Profit Potential: _____

Sell Transaction

Date: _____ Stock Price: _____

Number of Shares: _____ Minus Commission: _____

Price per Share: _____ Amount Received: _____

Why you sold the stock: _____

_____

Profit or Loss Percentage

Amount Received: _____

Purchase Price: _____

Profit or Loss: _____

Divide Profit or Loss by Purchase Price to get the Percent

_____

Percent Profit or Loss: _____

What you learned from this transaction:._____

_____

Stock Price Data Worksheet

52 Week High	Low	Company Name	Date Purchased	Price Per Share

Day or Week	Price per Share	Up or Down	Day or Week	Price Per Share	Up or Down
1			21		
2			22		
3			23		
4			24		
5			25		
Percent Change		%	Percent Change		
6			26		
7			27		
8			28		
9			29		
10			30		
Percent Change		%	Percent Change		
11			31		
12			32		
13			33		
14			34		
15			35		
Percent Change		%	Percent Change		
16			36		
17			37		
18			38		
19			39		
20			40		
Percent Change		%	Percent Change		

Selling Price: _____

Chapter

16

Lessons Learned

This final chapter offers the opportunity to test just how much you have learned. I have already covered diverse topics, such as how to find potential investments, how to analyze them, the positive and negative aspects that can affect a stock's profit potential, tips for buying and selling your stock for the best profit, locating the right broker for your needs and how to avoid stock scams. The questions that follow cover some of the facts you should know. The page number on the right hand side indicates where the answer can be found.

I wrote Making BIG Money in Small Stocks to help you become a wiser and more profitable investor. By investing the time to read and analyze this information, you have taken the first step. Applying this knowledge to your future investments will give you a more solid foundation for making smart investment decisions. You have the information; let's start making money now!

Glossary

accounts payable   A liability reflected under the "current" section of a balance sheet. It may include the total of amounts due within one year for the purchase of inventory or other direct costs, general overhead expenses and other amounts owed.

ADR   American Depositary Receipt is a receipt in the form of a certificate for U.S.-traded securities representing stock in foreign corporations.

annual report   The yearly financial statement of a corporation's financial condition. The report shows assets, liabilities and earnings, as well as a description of the company's operations, how it stood at the close of the business year, how it fared in terms of profit and other information of interest to shareholders.

Amex   The American Stock Exchange is ranked second behind the NYSE in most stringent requirements for listing.

asked   The lowest price that is acceptable to a seller of a security at a particular time. Price that a potential shareholder would have to pay to buy stock in that security.

asset   Any item of value that is owned by a business, institution or individual.

balance sheet   A condensed financial statement providing a picture of a company's assets, liabilities and capital on a given date.

bear   Someone who believes the market will decline.

bear market   A declining market in stocks usually brought on by anticipation of declining economic activity.

bid   The highest price a prospective buyer is prepared to pay at that specific time for a security. Price that a shareholder would receive if they sold the stock.

Blue chip stock   Shares of a company known for the quality and wide acceptance of its products or services with a steady record of profit growth and dividend payouts and a high probability of continued growth and future growth.

blue-sky laws   The popular name for laws enacted by various states to protect the public against securities fraud.   The term is said to have originated from a judge who asserted that a particular stock had about as much value as a patch of blue sky.

book value   Determined by the total assets of a company, minus liabilities and preferred stock. The sum is divided by the number of outstanding common stock shares.

broker   An individual who acts as an agent in the buying and selling of investments.

bull   Someone who believes the market will rise.

bull market   A rising stock market. Usually lasting at least a few months, bull markets are characterized by large trading volume.

capital gain or capital loss   The profit or loss difference between the purchase and sale price of an investment.

cash flow   An accounting term describing the positive or negative effect on cash generated from operations. It is the net income of a corporation plus amounts charged off for depreciation, depletion, amortization, etc.

certificate   A document proving ownership of a security. It usually is finely engraved with delicate etchings on watermarked paper to discourage forgery.

churning   A practice of overactive trading of customer accounts to generate commission income for the broker rather than to make a profit for the customer.

closely held corporation   Any corporation in which a substantial portion of the voting shares is held by a small number of shareholders.

closing price   Price at which a security trades at the close of the day.

collateral   Securities or other assets pledged by a borrower to guarantee repayment of a loan.

commission   The broker's fee for buying or selling a security.

common stock   Securities representing an ownership interest in an incorporated enterprise. Common stockholders have a residual claim on earnings and assets after all debt and preferred stock obligations have been met.

conflict of interest   A situation in which an individual who has control, influence or authority over a company may personally benefit from actions or decisions made by that company.

conglomerate   A corporation that has diversified its operations, usually by acquiring enterprises in widely varied industries.

Consumer Price Index (CPI)   Published by the Department of Labor, this index measures the prices of consumer goods and services.

convertible   A bond, preferred share or debenture that may be exchanged by the owner for common stock.

current assets   A company's tangible assets that are held in the form of cash or any other form that could be converted to cash within one year.

current liabilities   A company's debts that are due and payable within one year.

day order   A type of buy or sell order that is valid only for a single trading day.

debenture   A promissory note backed by the general credit of a company and usually not secured by a mortgage or lien on any specific property.

depreciation   A bookkeeping entry. Normally, charges against earnings to write off the cost, less salvage value, of an asset over its estimated useful life.

dilution   A decrease in the percentage of ownership in a corporation to an individual shareholder when more shares are issued to other shareholders.

discount broker   A broker offering only services to buy or sell securities. The commission is cheaper because he or she gives no investment consultation, advice, literature or other support.

discount rate   The interest rate charged by the Federal Reserve System on loans to member banks.

diversification   Spreading investments among different types of securities, companies, industries and risks.

dividends   Payments made by companies to their stockholders, usually from profits.

dollar cost averaging   A system of buying securities at regular intervals with a fixed-dollar amount, rather than purchasing a specific number of shares or units.

Dow   Usually refers to the Dow Jones Industrial Average, the most commonly used stock market index.

downtick   A transaction made at a price lower than the previous transaction.

due diligence   A thorough investigation of a company that is preparing to go public, undertaken by the company's underwriter and accounting firm.

earnings per share   The amount of net income earned per share of common stock after payment of dividends to preferred shareholders.

earnings report   Also called income statement. It reports a company's earnings or losses over a given period.

effective date   The date when a registered offering may be sold to the public.

exchange   An organized marketplace in which stocks, common stock equivalents and bonds are traded by members of the exchange, acting both as brokers and dealers/traders.   Through exchanges, brokers and dealers meet to execute orders from institutional and individual investors and to buy and sell securities.

face value   The par value of a bond, printed on the face of the certificate, indicating the amount the issuer promises to pay on maturity.

firm commitment underwriting   Where an investment banker commits its capital by buying the securities outright, becoming the owner of all securities that are not resold to the public.

fiscal year   A 12-month business year chosen by an organization for tax and financial reporting.   The fiscal year may end at any month.

float   Shares of a security available for buying or selling.   Shares in the public hands as opposed to closely held.

forms 10-K and 10-Q   Reports filed with the SEC by all listed corporations.   The 10-K is an annual report, and the 10-Q is a quarterly report.

fundamental analysis   The evaluation of a company by studying its management, financial and competitive positions.

going public   Offering securities to the public for the first time.

Gross Domestic Product (GDP)   Formerly called the gross national product, the GDP is a measure of a nation's total output.   It is the value of goods and services bought and sold, including personal consumption, government purchases, investment in business equipment and the net difference between foreign purchase of American exports and domestic purchase of foreign imports.

growth stock   A stock with a record of rapid growth or the potential for rapid growth.

Holding company   A corporation that owns the securities of another, in most cases with voting control.   A holding company may be formed to manage and control several related companies.

hot issue   A security about to be offered for sale that has generated extreme interest and should trade above the public offering price.

hype   To promote a stock with misleading or inaccurate information.

inactive stock   A stock that trades a very low volume of shares. Many inactive stocks are traded in 10-share units rather than the customary 100-share units.

income statement   A financial statement providing a picture of the company's interim earnings, such as total revenues, costs, expenses and net earnings from operations.

inflation   The economic environment in which prices rise, resulting in a decline in the buying power of the dollar.

initial public offering (IPO)   A company's first sale of stock to the public. Companies seeking outside equity capital and a public market for their stock will make an initial public offering.

inside information   Company affairs that have not been made public. It is illegal to use inside information on, for example, a takeover attempt or greatly changed earnings to buy or sell stock for a profit.

insider   An officer or director of a corporation, anyone who owns 10 percent or more of a company's voting stock or an individual with inside information.

institutional investor   An organization whose primary purpose is to invest its own assets or those held in trust by it for others. It trades in high volumes, receiving discounted commissions for block trading.

interest   The payment a borrower makes to a lender for the use of the lender's money.

investment   Using money to make more money; to gain income or increase capital or both.

investment adviser   An individual who provides financial consultation. The title is used by financial planners, registered investment advisers and securities and insurance salespeople.

investment banker   Another term for an underwriter or any person or firm helping a corporation issue new securities.

investment company   A company whose sole purpose is to earn income by investing the pooled capital of many other investors in other corporations.

IPO (initial public offering)   The initial public offering of a stock to the investing public.

issue   Any of a company's securities or the act of distributing such securities.

junk bond A bond with a speculative rating of BB or lower by Standard & Poor's and Moody's rating systems. The ratings range from AAA (highly unlikely to default) to D (in default).

leverage The technique of using borrowed funds or special types of securities (warrants, calls) in an attempt to increase the rate of return on investment. While the rate of return using leverage is greater, the risk to the investor is also increased because the principal and specified rate of interest must be repaid.

liabilities All obligations or debts owed by a corporation.

limit order An order to buy or sell a security (if it is possible) at a specified price.

liquidation The process of converting securities or other property into cash.

liquidity The ease with which an investment can be converted to cash.

listed stock The stock of a corporation listed on one of the major exchanges. To become listed and maintain that listing, a corporation must meet certain criteria.

load The sales charge assessed against investors in mutual funds, direct participation and other investment programs. The load usually covers sales commissions and all other distribution costs.

manipulation Buying or selling a security for the purpose of creating the false or misleading appearance of active trading. The creation of an artificial price movement, either up or down, to induce the purchase or sale of the security by other investors.

margin Buying securities with a percentage of the purchase price borrowed through the brokerage firm.

market maker A dealer on the NASDAQ exchange who maintains firm bid and offer prices in a particular security by standing ready to buy or sell round lots at publicly quoted prices.

market order Order to buy or sell a security at the best available price.

market price The current or last reported price for which a security traded.

municipal bond Tax-free bonds issued by state and local governments.

NASD National Association of Securities Dealers is a self-regulatory agency for brokers and dealers in the NASDAQ securities business.

NASDAQ National Association of Securities Dealers Automated Quotations system is an information network providing price quotations on securities traded on the system.

NASDAQ Composite Index   A measure of the aggregate performance of all NASDAQ/NMS stocks (except warrants) and all other NASDAQ domestic common stocks.   It is a market-value-weighted index – the influence of each stock on the index is proportionate to its price times the number of shares outstanding.

net income   The profits from company operations. Net income may mean actual income either before or after deducting applicable federal income taxes.

net worth   Assets minus liabilities.   Total shareholder's equity in a corporation.

new issue   The sale of a stock or bond that has not previously been offered by a corporation.

NYSE   *The New York Stock Exchange* is the world's most prestigious investment trading market and has the highest standards for stock listing.

NYSE composite index   The composite index of all stocks listed on the New York Stock Exchange, weighted by the number of shares outstanding and reporting the change in value. The index assigns a dollar value to that change to indicate relative movements.

odd lot   A stock trade of fewer than 100 shares. Round lots are traded in groups of 100 or multiples of 100 shares.

offer   The price at which a security is offered for sale. (Same as asked price.)

open order   An order to buy or sell securities that has been given but is not yet concluded. It can be closed in three ways: cancellation, execution or expiration.

option   The exclusive right to buy or sell property or securities at a specified price within a specified time. An option usually has a much shorter time period than a warrant.

Over the Counter   Securities traded among broker-dealers and not through listings on an exchange. Securities include those of corporations that do not meet the listing criteria of the NYSE or Amex exchanges, government and municipal debt securities and the securities of many financial service companies (banks, insurance companies, etc.). Name recently changed to NASDAQ.

paper profit or loss   An unrealized profit or loss on a security caused by the price either moving upward or downward from the investor's purchase price. Paper profits or losses become real only when the security is sold.

par value   The dollar amount assigned to a common share by the company's charter. Par value has little significance as far as the market value of common stock is concerned.

penny stocks   Low-priced issues, often highly speculative, selling for less than $1 per share. Often used as a derogatory term. A few penny stocks have grown into exceptionally high-quality companies.

pink sheets   Over-the-Counter securities that do not have a stock symbol. Pink-sheet stocks can be very speculative, with large spreads between the bid and asked prices.

portfolio   An individual's or institution's securities holdings. A portfolio may contain bonds, preferred stocks and common stocks of various types of enterprises.

preferred stock   Like common stock, except usually without voting rights. However, specified dividends are paid to preferred shareholders before dividends are paid on the common shares.

price-earnings ratio   A stock's market price divided by earnings per share for a 12-month period. A low PE ratio is considered relatively safe but less likely to increase in value in a bull market. A high PE ratio indicates greater risk and volatility.

primary market   The initial market for the distribution of securities. After the initial sale, they are traded in the secondary market.

producer price index   Formerly called the wholesale price index, the PPI measures wholesale inflation.

profit taking   Selling a stock that has gone up in value since its purchase in order to realize the profit. Profit taking is often the cause of a downturn in the market following a period of rising prices.

prospectus   The official selling circular that all companies offering new securities for public sale must file with the SEC. The prospectus offers detailed information about the company's financial position, planned use of the new funds and the qualifications of the corporate officers, etc.

proxy   A signed authorization by a shareholder allowing someone else to represent him or her and vote his or her shares at the shareholders' meeting.

proxy fight   The attempt by a group of shareholders to obtain enough votes to replace a corporation's management or overrule it on specific decisions.

proxy statement   The SEC-required statement of information about the items being voted on, which must be given to shareholders when a solicitation for a proxy is mailed.

public offering   The sale of securities to the general public.

quotation or quote   The highest bid to buy and the lowest offer to sell a security at a specific time. If your broker gives you a quote on a stock as $1.50 to $1.75, it means that if you wish to buy stock it would cost you $1.75 per share; however, if you wish to sell stock, you would receive $1.50 per share.

rally   A sudden and unexpected increase in market value, either in the stock market as a whole or a particular industry or security.

random walk   A theory of market behavior that states that the price of securities cannot be determined but is entirely random.

regional exchanges   Stock exchanges that serve distinct regions, such as Philadelphia, Pacific, Boston, Chicago, etc.

registration   Before a new security can be offered to the public, the security must be registered under the Securities Act of 1933. The company must disclose pertinent information relating to its operations, securities and management.

reverse split   The reduction of the total number of shares outstanding by reissuing shares at a higher par value. A reverse stock split is usually bad news for shareholders.

rights   The opportunity (at the company's discretion) for shareholders to acquire new stock at a specified price and in relation to the number of shares currently held.

round lot   The basic unit in which stocks are traded. For most securities, this is 100 shares.

Schedule 13D   A Schedule 13D must be filed with the SEC by any person who purchases or acquires 5 percent or more of the securities in any corporation registered with the SEC.

SEC   The Securities and Exchange Commission is a federal agency with direct regulatory authority over the securities industry.

secondary market   A market in which securities can be bought and sold by the public, following an initial offering.

sell order   An order given by a customer to a broker-dealer to liquidate (sell) a security on the market.

shareholders' meeting   The annual meeting held by a public company to give shareholders a voice in company actions.

shares outstanding   The number of a corporation's shares that are owned by the public (including management) and not held by the corporation in its treasury.

short sale   A form of speculation in which the price of a stock is expected to decline. Securities are bought and sold and are later bought back at the lower price.

SIPC   Securities Investors Protection Corporation is a government sponsored, nonprofit organization that insures customer cash and securities on deposit with a member securities firm.

specialist   A member of the NYSE who acts as a broker in the execution of orders and as a dealer by transacting for his or her own account. The specialist maintains an orderly market in the stocks for which he or she is registered as a specialist.

speculating   Purchasing high-risk, volatile investments with the hope of realizing large returns.

spread   The difference between the bid (the price at which a Market Maker will buy a security) and the asked (the price at which a Market Maker will sell a security) price. The spread narrows or widens according to the supply and demand for the security being traded.

stock limit order   An order to buy or sell a security when its price reaches a certain level.

stock split   Dividing a company's existing stock into more shares and reducing the price per share to improve the marketability of the shares. Also called a forward split.

stop loss order   An order to sell a security if a certain price is reached. Used to protect profit.

stop order   An order to sell at a price below or buy at a price above the current market.

street name   Securities kept in the name of a broker instead of the customer who actually owns the stock. This occurs when the securities have been bought on margin or when the customer wishes the security to be held by the broker.

syndicate   A group of investors who agree to raise capital to purchase the securities of an issuer. Also referred to as an underwriter.

takeover   The acquiring of one company by another.

target company   A company that is the subject of a takeover attempt by another company.

tax loss carry-forward   A tax provision allowing losses to be claimed in the years after the loss occurs. Can be used to offset profits so less tax is owed.

tender offer   A public offer to purchase shares of a corporation from existing shareholders. The tender offer specifies a price and time period for the offer.

third market   Trading of stock exchange-listed securities in the NASDAQ market by non exchange member brokers and all types of investors.

ticker   Instruments that display both the volume and price of security transactions worldwide. Nowadays the display is usually computerized; years ago it was on ticker tape.

tip   Advice to buy or sell a stock made on supposedly "inside" information.

underwriter   Usually an investment dealer who agrees to buy all or part of a new-issue security from a company with the expectation that the security can be resold to the public.

unit   A minimum amount of common stocks, warrants or other securities that are accepted for trading on an exchange. New-issue stocks may offer a unit composed of various amounts of common stock, warrants or other securities.

uptick   A transaction made at a price higher than the preceding transaction.

volatility   A measure of price movement in a security, industry or entire market.

volume   The number of shares traded by either a specific security or a whole market for a given period of time.

warrant   A certificate giving the holder the right to buy securities at a specific price, usually within a particular time period. When a stock's price is higher or expected to be higher than the warrant's specified purchase price, then the warrant has a market value and is frequently traded.

yield   The return on an investment expressed as a percentage of the current price.

Share *Making BIG Money in Small Stocks*
with friends, family and colleagues

YES, please send _____ gift **autographed** copies of *Making BIG Money in Small Stocks* to those listed below for the special price of **$31 per copy, a savings of more than 20%** off the normal bookstore price of $39.95.

PLUS send one autographed copy **FREE**, one for every four paid copies. I understand you will ship every copy absolutely **FREE!**

☐ **Enclosed is my check for $ _____** (**$31 x number of books**)
  Illinois residents add 8.25% sales tax
☐ **Charge my** ☐ **Visa** ☐ **MasterCard** ☐ **Discover**

Name: _____ Daytime Phone: _____

Address: _____

City/State/Zip: _____

Credit Card #: _____ Exp Date: _____

Signature: _____

Mail orders to: Mathews & Associates, Inc., 2549 West Golf Road, Suite 350, Hoffman Estates, IL 60194
Call 1-847-697-5666 today and place your order
Or fax your order to 1-847-697-5699.
Website: www.bigmoneysmallstocks.com

Please send a gift copy of *Making BIG Money in Small Stocks* to:

Name: _____

Address: _____

City/State/Zip: _____

Gift From: _____ Autograph to: _____

Send the book to me and I will deliver: ☐

Name: _____

Address: _____

City/State/Zip: _____

Gift From: _____ Autograph to: _____

Send the book to me and I will deliver: ☐

There's more order blanks on the reverse side –

Buy 4 books and receive a 5th one FREE

Buy 4 books and receive a 5th one FREE

Save more than 20% off the normal bookstore price of $39.95. Just fill in the names and addresses of those you want to receive *Making BIG Money in Small Stocks*. Then mail this form along with a check (or use your credit card).

Mathews & Associates, Inc., 2549 West Golf Road, Suite 350,

Hoffman Estates, IL 60194

Call 1-847-697-5666 today and place your order

Or fax your order to 1-847-697-5699.

Please send a gift copy of *Making BIG Money in Small Stocks* to:

Name: _____

Address: _____

City/State/Zip: _____

Gift From: _____ Autograph to: _____

Send the book to me and I will deliver: ☐

Name: _____

Address: _____

City/State/Zip: _____

Gift From: _____ Autograph to: _____

Send the book to me and I will deliver: ☐

Special Bonus: This copy is FREE (with four paid orders)

Name: _____

Address: _____

City/State/Zip: _____

Gift From: _____ Autograph to: _____

Send the book to me and I will deliver: ☐

Thank you for your order!

Website: www.bigmoneysmallstocks.com